NorthPoet

–

Just Ask The Ravens

–

JK Salmon

–

CONTENTS

IN THIS GREAT WILDERNESS

You come to me,
graceful from the edge
of the world, you come to me,
here in the heart of winter & the great
sleeping solitude of the Earth,
you come to me & I suddenly remember
each kiss & caress still shimmering, in the embrace
of Spring & the blossoms of a thousand mystic Lovers,
you make me remember & somehow take me dancing,
in the slow sensual intensity of your eyes,
you come to me & suddenly I can breathe,
at least for a moment, the fragrance of the Cosmos
laughing amid the blossoms, you come to me, so subtle,
gentle & profound, silent when the world grows clamorous
& graceful in your gestures, it seems you have always been here,
watching, waiting & softly wary, as if you knew Love
was quietly stirring, somewhere amid the snowflakes
& my constant backward glances, you smile & the shadows
warm with whispers, who you are I truly know not, except
that you are as relentless as the galaxies & as enduring as nebulae,
in your gaze I sense the mysteries of the great river who guides us all,
I know Life flows to sure & certain purpose & Ecstasy is real,
deeper than the heartbeat, purer than the longing of whispers
except when Rapture guides them, I know you reveal
the perfect dewdrop of the moment, fragile
in this great wilderness of my Spirit,
quivering with Rebirth, & the exquisite
taste of trembling lips...

1

WONDROUS GRACE

Just
let me lie
gentle beside you
& hear you breathing,
just let me lie naked in your arms
& you in mine, skin to skin
& heartbeat to heartbeat, just let me
dream beside you & somehow kiss you,
deep in the rapture where only our Spirits dance,
just let me hold you as if a miracle,
fleeting as the Cosmos & constant as a tear,
tonight is ours & all the erotic scents of midnight,
just let me lie here beside you & drift in the subtle dances
of Moonlight that flicker across your skin,
just let me know you deeper than this mere ecstasy of the flesh,
just let me mingle with your fragrance
& the shining of your atoms, let me hear your whispers
as our bodies grow subtly incandescent & our touch electrifies,
let me sail you like the tide that never ceases,
like the ocean deeper than the Earth,
here we are & tonight that's everything, your eyes
are the eyes of galaxies & the nebulae tingle in our bones,
we were here, we loved & somehow touched the Magic,
just let me lie beside you, immanent with flame,
just let me lie & hear you breathing,
& trace the outline of your cheek bones
with a touch of wondrous
Grace...

THE GROUND BENEATH YOUR ROOTS

I'll
just meet you,
here on the other side of Chaos,
I'll just call you, here amid the nectar
of all lost & forgotten blossoms,
I'll just be here, with large & mystic eyes,
I'll just meet you, dancing by the waves,
aglow in the kaleidoscope of ancient beacons,
I'll just whisper, here beside the flame that always shimmers
with the ghost of Stars wild across the meadows,
I'll just be here, amorous & amoral,
waiting for the last night of the constellations,
I'll just be here to guide you home, blue of eye
& dangerous of dream, I'll just strain each muscle & bend my back,
as if to support the galaxies at least a moment,
as if this was the last loving & terrifying moment when we
meet each other naked beneath the exquisite fingers of the Moon,
I'm just here to Love you & ravish you & shelter you in each
great rising of the Wind, in each searing conjuring of the Storm,
just embrace me before you forget me,
before we both smile & become the river ripe with nebulae,
before tomorrow sweeps us somehow back to yesterday
when instinct was all we had, bright in the opening of golden wings
& the endless blessing of the Sun,
just remember me & recognize me, at last & then forever,
just meet me here on this sacred ground
where the trees still shiver with mystic Light,
just come to me open & in Rapture, as if a Goddess & a maiden,
I'm just waiting here for redemption, I'm proud but you can bend me,

just gather me to dewdrops & I will be your oak,
ever ready to embrace you, ever ready
to guard you fiercely, like the ground
beneath your roots...

THE MAGIX OF QUEEN KATHERINE

Here I am,
& it's all I ever will be,
here I am, & tomorrow will unfold
as certain as yesterday, here I am,
ancient, invincible, immortal in each subtle
rising of the leaves, here I am, asleep
but almost trembling in Spring's bright anticipation,
I will be here, always dancing quietly in the corner of your eye,
here I am, born to kiss you, born to serve you, born to reveal you
to the Stars, here I am & the morning always calls me,
just a moment before the dawn, when phantoms sigh & mix
with the dreams of Lovers, here I am & here is the Moonlight,
poised & breathless on the Beauty of yet another precipice,
here we are, quietly ecstatic & vibrant in our limbs,
here we are no matter where the Fates may cast us, here we are,
breathless, naked, newborn & yet as ancient as the first
amorous whisper of the Cosmos, each winter seems to wound us
& our bodies fade away, invisible into the nebulae,
storms & the sweet cleansing of the rain seem to return our atoms
to the murmurs of the Earth, each snowflake seems to send us
to the serenity that has no name, but then the comets come
& the electricity of Midnight, our devotion is forever, to our Heartbeat
& the galaxies who cast us, here among the humans & the Mystery
of our eyes, here we are, human & ever hopeful, here we kiss,
& embrace in a thousand meadows, ephemeral as the blossoms,
but always enduring, here we are, awash in Magic,
deep in the eyes of nebulae, & tasting of youth
& endless summers...

SILENTLY, IN YOUR BEAUTY

I was
always the secret
I never quite revealed, I was
always the secret, the Mystery, the Magic
of a fleeting moment, I was always
the Moonlight, the erotic stirring of the Stars,
I came to you & I knew the thousand Magics
you held hidden in your heartbeats, I was the secret,
the Magic & the conjuring, the shiver of the breeze at midnight,
the erotic tapping at your window, look for me
where phantoms glide, sensuous across the meadows,
I was the madness, the mayhem & the strange fruit
of amorous orchards, I dance where no tigers dance, I kiss
as if I knew our Spirits were infinite, as if I knew our flesh
was infinite & bright with atoms, come with me, Love,
to this strange beginning & ending of the worlds, tomorrow
is always as naked as the nebulae, raw with possibilities
& trembling with the infinities of desire, come closer & you'll hear me
singing, somewhere in the blossoms & the dangerous trembling
of the leaves, I hear the rising of the tides & the strange
wild laughter of the Cosmos, tomorrow is as fragile as the taste
of yesterday's rainbows, we're here & that's all that matters,
the Goddess endures & in you she endures & flourishes,
almost silently in your Beauty, as miraculous
& subtle as the Moonlight...

THE MOON ALWAYS NEEDS A HERO

I know
it all now, & I somehow
wish I didn't, I wish I'd listened
to at least a thousand of my Lovers,
I wish I'd been bigger, braver & more aware,
I wish I hadn't needed so much
& been so hungry, I wish I'd been high minded
& unswerving in my purpose,
I wish I'd been more grateful & the streets not quite
so crooked, I wish I'd never gone wild & come through smiling,
but the tides rose & the dangerous Stars promised
to always heal me, even among the ruins of the golden cities,
the Moon always needs a Hero & once I'd let you go I knew
the Midnight owned me, you think I'm lost but that's not quite true,
I know exactly where I am & that's in the graveyard
of all possible rainbows, I know why the Cosmos smiles
& that's because it loves me, somewhere in the cool glittering arms
of its constellations, all I wanted was the truth & the peace
of a gentle summer, fragrant across the meadows,
all I wanted was nothing except that it had some meaning
if you ever asked me, now all I am is human, no better & no worse,
the seasons call me, somewhere in the silence between my heartbeats,
I just rode forward, sometimes in tears & sometimes dancing,
I just drew the first exquisite electricity of my breath,
shining into the maelstrom of my atoms & that was it,
I was here in all my Magic
& fleeting glory...

EVANGELINE, IN RAPTURE

Once I was
always there for you,
once I was always there
& then I never was, I just somehow
lost you, mistake by mistake & heartache
by heartache, out on each burning bridge
beneath the Stars, I was always strong
but you were always stronger & wilder & purer,
you were always the miracle I struggled so hard to embrace,
each of your battles I fought beside you but your enemies
just grew stronger, like the dangers whose name were legion,
I always loved you with that long, lost & hopeless Love
all true pilgrims embrace, I knew each Midnight rising
of the storms that rattled the great glittering dreams
of the constellations, I knew the bread, the roses, the sacred wine
that almost freed you, I came riding, battered, bruised & bleeding,
to each of your disasters, to each of your whispers
that promised freedom, I came to you, I hungered,
I died a thousand times before your faith revived me,
before I finally found redemption just by loving you & letting you
slip through the last trembling of my fingers, I prayed for ecstasy
& the rapture to reach you just before the morning,
when the Earth shook off all mystery & bathed itself in rainbows,
I never truly believed you when you laughed & tossed each tenderness
to the wind, I knew you were broken & all hope had been forgotten,
I knew you were the Beauty for which there is no true name,
I knew the Cosmos would finally kiss you but it took me
a thousand years, to finally forgive the skyline
for each of your endless tears...

RAINBOWS IN BABYLON

I just wanted
to leave something,
gentle in your hand, something
precious & subtle with Magic,
I just wanted to reach you,
with a whisper & a kiss, from the far side
of every rainbow that once embraced us,
I just wanted to touch you, as if a cleansing raindrop
dancing but a moment on your lips,
I just wanted to empty my pockets & give you
every Star we ever dreamed of, I just
wanted to unravel each mystery of our touch,
each ecstasy of our atoms, I just wanted to flicker
with the strange electricity of long lost constellations
through the leaves that crackled with the coming of the frost,
I just wanted to sleep the long sleep with you even though
I went before you, I just wanted to reach you though the wind
scattered me like the dust of amorous yesterdays,
I just wanted to kiss you & know I somehow mattered,
at least for a moment, in the soft swirling river of your ecstasy,
I knew you once, when I stepped on the shore, battered, bloodied
& triumphant, when wisdom still shone hard won
& beautiful, I just wanted to leave you something, a gentle reminder,
that once was a knight & pure were the days, moments are best forgotten
& laughter is light & lingers in the Moonlight, I was here, I loved you
& then it ended, not because we wished it, but because
the Cosmos beckoned & tomorrow was fickle
& undefined...

A LILY OF ALL REDEMPTION

I came to you,
brave on the river,
I came to you, across the abyss
that opened in my Heart, I came to you,
like a knight disguised as a joker,
you never knew me except that you always did,
behind each subtle horizon of your eyes,
you knew me & saw right through me,
or at least you thought you did, in the jokes & the Magic
& the laughter, you thought you knew me
but that was just the phantoms smiling in the mirror,
I came to you & I came dancing, open handed & alone,
even on the arms of a thousand maidens,
it's true I loved you but I loved you perfectly, in spite of everything,
I just smiled & wept while I was laughing,
I knew you would rip me & lay me out bleeding
beneath the cruel sympathy of the Stars, I knew you would
rip me & not even notice the rainbows were burning,
I came to you on a river the Cosmos wept, in the meadows
of perfect dewdrops, I came to you beautiful in sunlight,
as if mysterious & wild, I came to you & I told you everything
& it was almost like you believed me, in that long lost time
that was only yesterday, I had the Magic & you had the shimmering skin,
I came to you in a moment that was perfect & in innocence
you redeemed me, smiling & unaware, I came to you
& Beauty released me, finally & forever, in our last & ultimate
moment, when everything was lost in the whisper of snowflakes
& all we did was embrace, I came & you caressed me,
with exquisite whispers & a promise
of peace...

A LOVER LINGERS

That's
just me knocking,
here on the edge of nowhere,
that's just me knocking,
here on the horizon, here on the edge
of my last & most exquisite breath,
that's just me knocking, almost joyous, almost tearful,
that's just me knocking & hoping & praying,
desperate to find you home, desperate to whisper
at least a fleeting moment in your ear,
that's just me with a thousand secrets, a thousand memories,
that's just me knocking, weapons already buried,
Heart already opened & tears scattered to the wind,
that's just me knocking with dew in my hair
& sunlight simmering in my Spirit, that's just me dancing,
smiling, weeping & triumphant, that's just me
aching to kiss you, to kindle the last & most subtle Flame,
that's just me here beneath the constellations
with the scent of Midnight on my skin, that's just me
finally singing, finally winged & embracing my dreams,
that's just me finally flying, finally shining, finally shimmering
with Grace, that's just me embracing the galaxies
& calling each nebulae by name, that's just me still honouring
my heartbeat & knowing Love lasts forever, that's just me knocking,
a moment before I'm gone, that's just me knocking,
that's just the innocence of childhood & the last laugh
lingering, entwined & joined
in Rapture...

A GREAT DELUGE OF RAINBOWS

I'll just wait here,
a thousand furies subsided
& finally peaceful, I'll just wait here,
almost childlike, almost fearful,
I'll just wait here, as if remembering
& suddenly expectant, I'll just wait here,
ears straining for the first & last sound & the great
rising of the waves, I'll just wait here, bruised, battered
& only quietly triumphant, I'll just wait here,
for the great reckoning & the rebirth of all mystic promises,
I'll just wait here for the great deluge of rainbows,
for the mystery & madness of the Cosmos descending,
I'll just wait here, green as the grasses & aching as the blossoms,
I'll just wait here, weapons already buried, I'll just be waiting,
glowing in each memory of a glorious & misspent youth,
I'll just wait here, lost in the melancholy of long lost songs
& the surge of new melodies rising, I'll just wait here as if each breath
I drew somehow mattered, as if the nebulae will greet me,
I'll just linger as if the breeze always at your window,
I'll just be the Hero each midnight always thought I could be,
I'll just be the Lover who always remembered, who knew the secrets
of the storms that swept the world, I'll just wait here & perhaps
for a moment I'll remember each exquisite & eternal promise,
it's getting dark & I almost welcome it, as if at last I'll shine,
no longer lost & languishing amid the Constellations,
the Grace is coming & I feel it, in the smallest thing,
in the trembling of the dewdrops, in the least of all
simple miracles, when dawn whispers
to the Light & Magic reclaims
the World...

12

WOLVES LIE LONELY

If in the end
this is all it comes to,
if this is the end & not even
a new beginning, if it was all just a Magic,
a Mystery that engulfed us & swept us away
to the fragile memory of loving Stars,
if tomorrow is uncertain & yesterday already shining
in the atoms, if each kiss was just an impulse,
an electricity briefly beloved of an amorous Cosmos,
then that's alright, that's what it is & I accept it,
all I wanted was a moment anyway, a flash of ecstasy & a rapture
that somehow transcended everything, I never asked for forever
& that's just as well because I never got it, I sought
the rainbow bridge & I found it, I transcended, I touched the nebulae,
the Earth released me & gave me to the galaxies,
I took you with me & it was the ride that swept like a storm
across the abyss of the endless waters, I took you & you took me
& our embrace shone like the beacon all pilgrims dream of,
broken & hopeless out in each dangerous desert of the Spirit,
you took everything & I would have given you more, I just came knocking
& you let me in, I was armed & you taught me peace,
you gave me Grace, you gave me peace & stilled the anger in my fingers,
all I built I built because of you, I became everything
but that was never enough to enfold you, you were a child
& I was a child & that was how it always should be,
innocence always triumphs & wolves
lie lonely on the mountains...

WHERE THE WILD ONES PLAY

Here I am,
out here still dancing,
still dangerous, still believing,
here I am & here I always will be,
a knight, a lover, a ghost in the twilight,
here I am & there you are, wild eyed & waiting,
freed at last from everything but the night, the wind & the Stars,
there you are, eager on the edge of eternity's first & final kiss,
you're so close I can almost feel you, in each delicious
shiver of your atoms, it's dark but never lonely out here
in the wilderness where only the wild ones play,
each silence has a sound & it whispers like the birth of thunder,
like the gathering of rain, just take everything & I will
give you even more, the Cosmos smiles & is inexhaustible,
the Moonlight shimmers & the blossoms shine crystalline
in each meadow of our imagination, let the Midnight come,
the madness, the Mystery, the fingertips amorous with newborn Light,
I'm just here dancing & there you are, poised on the edge
of the galaxies, naked to the great abyss that holds the oceans
& great waves of the nebulae, that strange small sound
you hear is just me knocking, wary but smiling slyly,
on the last & lonely bridge between our Spirits,
that's just me shivering, out here
amid the rainbows...

FIERCE GALAXIES

Just
remember me,
here on this last
& loneliest night of the Earth,
just remember me & I will come to you,
holding high my ancient lantern,
I will come, though the path be wild, uncertain & dangerous,
I will come, sailing the last of my Heartbeats
with the gossamer sails of the Stars,
all I need is the infinity between one rapture & the next,
all I need is the ecstasy of yet another breath
even though it burns the last of the rainbows,
all I need is Love & the faint whisper of summer through the trees,
all I need are the fierce galaxies of your eyes
& I will fly among them with a host of constellations
& the exquisite Light of Suns gathering on every horizon,
I fear nothing & chaos calls me brother, just call me, just believe,
just remember, tomorrow burns bright in each dawn of yesterday,
I'll come knocking, as sure & sly as I ever was, amorous in my intentions
& roguish in my ways, just wait for me, just linger O my Love,
but a little longer & we will again be dancing amid the blossoms
& the subtle fragrance of the orchards, no wave is too wild, no sea is
too unruly to keep me from meeting you here at last in the Magic,
in the murmurs of the Nebulae, just remember me
& I will come, bold, bright & beautiful
in the precious miracles
of our Eyes...

A FIST FULL OF DIAMONDS

I always remember,
here in the arms of Midnight,
I always remember & almost touch you,
dancing beneath the streetlights & the rain,
I almost reach you, eyes alive with Magic,
I almost reach you, there in the arms of jealous yesterdays,
I almost hear you knocking, at the door of each of my simple dreams,
I almost remember you as more than a phantom of the rainbows,
it's almost like the Cosmos finally sheds a tear & embraces me,
it's almost like the darkness becomes a friendly enemy,
still dangerous but forgiving, I always remember & it's almost like
each breath was exquisite, like each dream was real,
tomorrow the oceans will break yet again upon the rocks
& grey will be the mists with each endless sorrow lingering,
but tonight nothing is impossible & even tomorrow smiles,
slyly in the shadows, tonight I remember & the Earth still loves me,
the scents of Spring still wander lightly through the orchards,
tonight I'm still innocent & I remember when I bartered our Stars
for a fist full of diamonds, regrets are useless & so are tears,
only the rains will cleanse me, wild with the caress of waves
rising to shake the world...

THAT LAST SWEET SONG

Just take me,
wherever you yet
linger a moment on this planet,
just take me & release me
from this burden of fear, delight & danger,
just take me, just reveal me, just meet me
in the ecstasy of each rainbow above the mountains,
just kiss me, with the taste of a thousand ecstasies,
with the flavour of rebirth & the miracle
of broken dreams made whole, just come to me
& cradle me, like the first & last of your Lovers,
like your Hero who still shines beneath the Stars in pure
but battered armour, strip me of everything, every dream,
every anger, every ecstasy that rippled across my atoms,
just remember me & come to me dancing,
in the fields we once entered so freely, as if the Earth's
beloved children, just come to me & heal me & kiss my brow,
for I am a fool in the grip of wisdom, a rogue released
& a rascal unbound, just take me with you to the arms of the Cosmos
& the miracle of electric fingers, tingling with the nebulae,
just touch me & release me, to the sea of miracles still shining
in my bloodstream, just remember me, here huddled confused & alone,
where the crossroads meet & the shadows just laugh & drive hard bargains,
just sing me that last sweet song that tells me it all had meaning,
that flesh & blood had purpose, that each breath was
somehow sacred & still shines, at least a moment
in constellations...

SWEET SAVANNAH

All
I wanted
was to Love you,
to touch you, lightly
on your Spirit & gently on your skin,
all I wanted was to be brave enough to reach you,
strong enough to hold you,
all I wanted was to dance there beside you,
in the last & most beautiful Midnight of the world,
all I wanted was the constellations,
exquisite & alive, electric in my fingers as I laid them
in your hair & crowned you with our dreams,
all I wanted was to kiss you, like a stranger coming home,
like a hero, like a Poet who somehow
swam amid the Stars, all I wanted was to breathe
the mystic scent of the meadows when we knew the comets
were alive, all I wanted was the Magic of your atoms,
exquisite & mingling with my own,
tomorrow never beckoned so I knew it was tonight,
as if each breath was infinite, as if we somehow lived forever
in each fleeting miracle of dawn's far flung blossoms,
you drove into the mountains & I knew the Moon would claim you,
I knew your whispers would have to last forever, in this
suddenly grey & untethered world, I knew no touch was infinite
except between our heartbeats, I knew the night would last forever
but dawn was mysterious in your eyes, you were the sunlight in me,
the tiny miracle, the ecstasy the Earth always granted,

to each true & loving madman, & each lost & lingering soul,
I knew you were gone & so was that strange peace
that almost claimed me, for a moment
in your Eyes...

A TENDRIL OF REBORN GREEN

I feel you,
in the first faint
stirring of the leaves,
I feel you & I know the blossoms
are already trembling, closer now,
aching for the Cosmos & the ecstasy of the dew,
I feel you coming, shining in the sunlight,
only as yet imagined, hair electric,
sensual, sacred & reborn in Spirit, flesh & bone,
I sense you shimmering, lightly across the frozen ecstasy
of the waters, I feel your breath, lightly against my ear,
whispering the incantation of youth
& eternal summers naked in each footstep of the Goddess,
I feel you coming, reborn from the ashes of winter's last wild bonfire,
I feel you yearning, tender as a tendril of reborn Green,
sensual, Magic, calling from the mountain, still dancing, still believing,
I feel you opening into wonder, into Mystery, into Life,
I hear you & I know what you are offering,
the treasure & the trembling Rapture of each of your exquisite breaths,
I want you & that's just the start of it, I want you
waiting, wary, innocent, in the meadows of infinite rainbows,
I know the galaxies & I know how quick they gather,
when the Cosmos spreads electric fingers & bequeaths them to the Earth,
I knew you were chained once & broken but so were we all,
in the first fury of love, lust & innocent danger,
your pain was just the baptism of ecstasy, dancing across the meadows
& long lost to memories, I know who you are & what

your real name is, when the nebulae gather in each of your secrets
& you wonder where the teardrops went,
when Bliss enfolds you & each of your atoms
seems exquisite...

WHERE MAGIC IS ALIVE

I always
come back,
to this wild old place,
to this haunted orchard & broken
landscape, I always come back
because my bones ache to lie a moment here,
or a Moonlit eternity when the last night comes,
I always come back & my Heart
beats stronger, my muscles tighten & my eyes
brighten & see what the eagles see,
I always come back & the grass quivers beneath my boots,
urging me onward, urging me to dance,
whispering of sloe eyed maidens & liquor fit for the gods,
I always come back, brash as a young man, last son
of the great blue ridged mountains, I always come back
& my Spirit soars, & that strange wild fire flickers
in my bloodstream again, like the caress of constellations,
like the ecstasy of Light across the waters, I always come home,
here to this forgotten place, to this forest of Dreams
& youthful Rapture, I always come back & it seems
I will never leave, here where the Magic is alive & smiles
with savage Grace, it's here I know I'll always find you,
sweet smiled & breezes blowing in your hair, it's here
all battles cease & all highways end, here where
Spring first rises, year after year & breath after breath,
eternal through the seasons,
& miraculous in hue...

UNCHAINED YESTERDAYS

Just
lay it down,
that ache, that heartbreak,
that darkness edging
into Light, just lay it down
& come forth shining, dancing
in this world of endless meadows,
in this roar of waves where horizons beckon,
just come forth & uncage each lost & loving yesterday,
youth has its chains, golden though they be,
each sweet breeze, each fragrant toss of sunlit hair
lingers but a moment though memory always wonders,
just come forth brave, bright eyed & beautiful,
just come forth & embrace this ecstasy of rising Spring,
just come forth naked & newborn, like a song of endless mornings
& the Rapture of the blossoms, just come forth trembling,
shimmering with dew's thousand promises,
just come forth & meet me bravely, lost in the joy & wonder of it all,
in the electricity of each fingertip, in the exhilaration
of each breath, I loved you once & then forever, but here
the Love is endless & shimmers in the wide open arms
of a boundless Cosmos, just lay it down, that burden, that Midnight
aching for lesser Stars, here all Dreams are infinite,
& exquisite in each whisper, here the wind steals all seasons
& gathers them in rainbows, here the storms are wild but the rain
cleanses gently, each lost & weary Spirit, each blade of grass tingling

with the miracle of our heartbeats, once so young & sensuous,
like nomads called by comets to climb
the mountains & await the coming
of adventure...

YEARNING FOR CONSTELLATIONS

I'll
just rest here,
perhaps
until the end of time,
I'll just rest here, & patiently wait,
because I know you're coming,
I'll just rest here & watch the mountains
crumble atom by atom & stone by stone,
I'll just wait here until yesterday stops hunting me,
until memories fade & my dreams return,
I'll just rest here, until the Silence seeps into my heartbeat
& I can finally hear all things, I'll just wait here
until you find me, until you reach me & redeem me,
I'll just wait here until my eyes are clear & my bones are golden,
I'll just wait until you Love me, until you come to me
in rainbows & the wild whispers of the wind,
I'll just wait until you kiss me, somewhere in the raindrops,
until the Earth embraces me with the innocence of your arms,
I renounce all anger, desire & pain, I break each chain that bound me,
no matter how golden, I renounce my strength so invincible
it let you slip like a moonbeam through my fingers,
I renounce all dangers & hungry Beauties, I just wait here,
hoping for Mercy, aching for the trembling touch of Hope long fled
to vanishing horizons, I just wait here because at last I no longer
need you or expect you, except that I keep breathing & within me
there is a universe deep & open & empty,
& yearning for Constellations...

THE GODDESS IN YOUR EYES

I thought
I could forget you,
just for a moment, I thought
I was free & you were once again
merely mortal, I thought I could forget you,
but that was just a surface ripple
of my mind & not my heartbeat speaking,
I thought I could forget you & maybe I can
just long enough to catch my breath,
just long enough for the dawn to touch me
& draw back the veils from across the horizons,
I thought I could forget you but that was just
a moment's hesitation, a confusion of lost clouds
briefly clinging to my Spirit, I thought I could forget you
but all I had forgotten was the Goddess in your eyes
& the fragrance of your hair upon my pillow,
all I had forgotten was that you were golden & shimmered
with all the hues of cleansing rain, all I'd forgotten
was the ocean always calling in the soft mystery of your whispers,
all I'd forgotten was our tent up in the mountains
& lying together in the grass, beside trees already imminent
with blossoms, I thought I was done with you, abandoned, broken,
& glad of it, I thought you were lost & just one more nomad Star
amid the constellations, I thought I could ride on, hard & holy in my armour,
but that was just a madman talking, a troubadour briefly
stumbling on his strings, as long as I live I will love you,
& the moments will seem like eons
until we kiss again...

EXQUISITE WRECKAGE

I remember you,
at the last & like the one
& only, I remember you,
with the peace that only comes
with the touch of dawn's faint first fingers,
I remember you, on this shore so suddenly
bereft of all familiar surroundings,
I remember you, here in this one lingering
& perfect moment, here in the exquisite wreckage
of each tsunami that swept away my world,
I remember you, here beneath these constellations
so suddenly unchained, I remember you, here, now, & perfectly forever,
I remember you, here in this universe of tears & tomorrow's
faint & already broken promises, I remember you & that's all
it comes to in the end, the sum total of each of my yearning heartbeats,
each of my hopeful & exquisite breaths, I remember you
as if the tents were already folding, as if the clowns had finally
all gone home, I remember you & I almost worship you,
as if my Life might actually have had some meaning & you were
the joyful Cosmos I danced within, who were you & why did I love you,
perhaps the sly wind knows but if so it forgot to tell me,
I'm just here, the last of the long lost knights still faintly glinting
beneath the battered constellations, I just remember you & that's
probably all I'll ever do, dance by dance & breath by breath,
like the ghost of long lost youth & the phantom who always haunts you,
amorous in the Midnight & whispering strange secrets,
fiercely in your ear...

SPRING IN SAVANNAH

Here I am,
in a Spring that won't
remember, in a memory
that still lingers, here I am, still as bold,
brash & beautiful but still
searching for the rainbows, here I am,
aching for a golden glimpse of you back
when our kisses mattered,
it happened so fast, the anger, the anguish,
the apocalypse of all once & future dreams,
I'm still here & you're still there, still wounded but still laughing,
somewhere in those sweet silver mountains of the Moon
we always conjured, skin to skin in the dances
of midnight summer meadows, here I am, not forgotten
but barely remembered, barely a ghost amid your host of brighter
phantoms, I came to you & you lit the thousand candles, the infinite ecstasy
of each of our sensuous atoms, where will you dance to now
with the music of our laughter so willfully forsaken,
I don't know & some days I barely care, I see you everywhere
but that's just wishful thinking, you're still there & I'm still here,
in a land of wilful dragons & monsters tingling in my veins,
I thought I was beyond all this, I thought I was stronger & wiser
& unflinching in my Spirit, but that was all yesterday,
when you wore a crown of constellations & we watched
the Sky from an ocean city, loving each
whisper of the waves...

AUTUMN'S RAINBOWS

I can't
forget you,
& I see you everywhere,
I can't forget you & my memories
always take me dancing,
the Moon hangs low & always
whispers in my ear, urging me onward,
turning me backward, leading me lost & lonely
into each back alley of regret,
I know each door to knock on, where sorrow
always dwells, I know each Magic, each pain,
each fond remembering, I almost think I see you but
then you're gone again, up to the mountains, down through
the valleys of useless regret, we are who we are & we did
what we did, foolishly but somehow forever,
each song we sang, each whisper, each Lover's promise
traced with trembling fingers on sensual skin, it's all just as fleeting
as last autumn's rainbows, it's dark here & the nights are cold,
the way is weary & the night seems long, I ache for the taste of midnight
& the exquisite flavours of your lips, I wonder where
the sunlight went & why the wild wind brought nothing but
the fiery flash of fading leaves, tomorrow just laughs at yesterday
& mocks my missing heartbeat, where are you tonight,
where do you wander & why, we were meant to be together,
at least a little longer while eternity spun around us, I believe in nothing
& I believe in everything, even the comfort of useless wisdom,
I'd do it all again & gladly, I'd kiss you just as fiercely,
I'd embrace you just as bravely,
I'd just never let you go...

WITH THE NEBULAE SINGING

There's
a thousand mountains,
watching, waiting, murmuring
sweet secrets only we will understand,
there's a thousand mountains
& a thousand peaceful valleys where we
may love in quiet ecstasy, gentle in the arms
of an amorous summer, there's a thousand hidden places,
deep in your body & in mine leading to
the natural Rapture of our senses, there's a thousand journeys,
each beginning with a single kiss beneath the Moonlight,
there's a touch, a taste, an embrace of hidden rainbows
always waiting to be discovered, there's the endless sound
of waves & the exquisite fragrances of Spring just rising,
there's the infinity of your eyes & the wild wind calling,
let us go, Love, let us embrace the dawn & our nomad heartbeats,
tomorrow is never easy but yesterday is gone,
I believe in the strength of new beginnings & the youth
of endless summers, here, right here where the Cosmos meets us
& mingles with our Spirits, I believe in the cool clear Light
of the constellations & the stories told by firelight,
it's all One & it's all Beautiful, the human & the holy,
I ache for you & I wait for you, here with the nebulae
singing, here with a thousand dreams
& Stars dancing in my eyes...

SARAH, ON THE SKYLINE

Perhaps
you've finally
come to me, easy, open
& beautiful, perhaps you've
finally come, smiling a secret smile
& all but unknowable in your Grace,
perhaps you've finally come,
reborn & quietly resplendent, as if subtly
dancing through the rainbows, perhaps you've
finally returned, demure as a maiden, fierce as kitten,
perhaps you're here & nothing will ever be the same,
no beauty, no sunset, no rise of evening Star,
all will be reborn, all will be renewed
& caught again in the arms of a loving Cosmos,
perhaps you're here & I was always waiting,
deep in the mists of memory, wild on the waves of yesterday
& endless tomorrows, all I have I bequeath you gladly, joyously,
as if you & you only could ever reach me in each dawn's
flickering promises, I don't know where you came from or where
you're going, except that you kiss me now, except that you embrace me
as chastely as a goddess, as amorously as each fleeting
ecstasy of the tides, I'll always be here, ageless & quietly waiting,
for each pleasure you always grant me, in our loving
conflagrations of flesh & blood & bone, tomorrow never matters,
nor the dangers of the wild wind blowing, fierce across
the waves rising to sweep away each world, just let me see your eyes,
soft, sensual & shimmering with each tear somehow sacred
to the skyline, just wait here beside me, gentle & genuine with mercy,
just electrify my fingers, with each tingle of our Spirits,
lost & somehow found...

31

A PROMISE OF CLEANSING RAIN

It always
comes to this,
that last long backward glance
& the sound of the river flowing,
it always comes to this,
here on the edge of tomorrow,
here where all things cling like the roots
& vines of yesterday or yearn like blossoms
toward the sunlight, it always comes to this,
one last useless battle & take up the Hero's crown,
or sail once more a pilgrim, trusting nothing & yet everything,
it always comes to this, alone amid the memories
already fast fading golden into mist, it always comes to this,
either heal yourself or stay bleeding, either embrace the Cosmos
or die a thousand deaths in a sea of relentless moments,
it always comes to this, a dawn of ecstatic possibilities
& Light breaking across the waters, all I ever wanted was nebulae
& rainbows shimmering in sensual midnights & the exquisite
embrace of summer meadows, all I ever wanted was the miracle
of your eyes & the truth of each loving prophecy,
all I wanted was to touch you with the subtle fingertips
of a Magic that always lingered, all I ever wanted
was Moonlight & the promise of cleansing rain
when each dusty day
was done...

A FLASH OF COMETS PASSING

Once
I almost loved you,
& sometimes I truly did,
once I almost loved you & that was
almost perfection, that was almost
the bliss I'd always longed for, the shelter
from the storm & the safe harbour
bright across the angry waters, once I truly loved you,
over & over & over again, in each conflagration
of the Rainbows, in each teardrop that somehow
swept away the world, once the Cosmos smiled & I knew
all the dances, once you laughed, lightly & with infinite longing,
as if all miracles awaited us, as if Magic was alive
& each electric touch was holy, once I lay with you
& Love almost seemed an easy thing, once Rapture shook us
& trembled with slow erotic fire in each breath we shared,
in each shiver of our golden bones, once I was bruised,
& broken & almost holy, once the Midnight knew the answers
& Moonlight caressed our skin, I'll never know
what happened, whether it all had meaning or was just the flash
of comets passing, I guess in the end it doesn't even matter,
I saw the galaxies rise, & each secret shudder of the nebulae
when ecstasy erupts into inconceivable Beauty,
come My Love, if I may call you that, let's just kiss & take
the west wind, each sail to a different world, once I almost loved you
& that was almost good enough, the rough ending made me human
& the ragged edges just make me your mystic scarecrow,
still restless in the cornfields & a plaything
for hungry crows...

A BRIEF FLICKER OF THE COSMOS DANCING

I no longer
remember, who
I am nor where, I no longer
remember nor do I care, as if my Life
has forgotten me & only the Stars
remember, yesterday vanishes, smiling
into the great ocean that slowly engulfs the world,
& all fleeting glory is the vanity of the wind,
the brief delicious chirping of sparrows
or grasshoppers who dance but in the miracle of a season,
all glory is vanity but Beauty Endures, Beauty lives on,
easily, inherent in the constellations, filling our divergent sails,
our hopes, our fears, our frenzied grasping fingers,
I was the brief flicker of the Cosmos dancing, the dream
of dangerous sunbeams gradually shown the Light,
at least remember me, if not as perfect then at least as perfectly
human, I was what I was & I forgive you completely
for each of your childish wanderings, for each misstep,
for each pain, each pinnacle we might have climbed together,
all was as it was & that was perfect in the end, your Eyes
were the Mystery always sensual in each Midnight sacred to
brief but courageous Lovers, let's just say our heartbeats entwined,
at least for the moment when it mattered, at least
for the great rising of the rainbows that finally consumed the Earth,
all things are One & that's the truth we need to cling to,
when Dawn comes slow & lonely,
& Magic is just a ruse...

WIDE & WONDROUS EYES

I never
drew any kind
of line in the sand for you,
& dared you to cross it,
I never drew any kind of line
& I never would, except for the pleasure
of watching you lightly laugh & leap above it,
I love you wild, I love you free & beloved
of the Cosmos, I don't even care if you take
a thousand Lovers, because I've had a thousand myself
over the years, I just want you with an ache
that's almost unendurable, with a yearning so bright
& beautiful it's almost like I don't even recognize myself in it,
I see the fools who love you, so full of fire & vanity,
I see the fools who love you & I wish them well,
I sympathize, I pity them, for this is your season of sensual power
& youthful glory, you're all I believe in, in a true way & a profound one,
the Earth is reborn, again & again, beloved of the Stars
& exquisite & shining, the Earth is reborn & the roots & blossoms
& ripe berries, the Earth is reborn & the fields & streams & dreams
& diaphanous shimmering of the dew, the Earth is reborn,
with each nebulae delicious in her eyes, it doesn't matter where,
when or why, it just is & I always feel it, I know who Spring belongs to
& whose atoms it ignites, just believe me & take these treasures
that I offer, a kiss is never enough but you bestow them freely
& my Spirit trembles with delight, each embrace threatens to consume me
but I crave the great awakening, the caress, the comets
& the rainbows, I just need you to be exactly as you are, mysterious
& seeking new adventures, sitting across the cafe table,
with wide & wondrous Eyes...

THESE SWEET & SIMPLE THINGS

This is
the one sweet secret
I never told you, the Magic
as yet unconjured, this is the one
sweet secret & the miracle unborn,
all things must pass & all winds must blow,
relentlessly across waves wild, unruly & flecked with Stars,
this is the touch, the whisper, the kiss tremulous
upon each of your secret places,
just listen & I will tell you what I learned,
a thousand lonely nights out in the wilderness
where beasts & strange phantoms impart their visions,
just listen & lie a little closer, just embrace me a moment
before midnight smiles set fire to the ecstasies of our atoms,
tonight is ancient & the Cosmos has dreamed it all before,
galaxy after galaxy, neuron after neuron,
the truth evolves & shimmers again & again in newfound Beauty,
tonight is naked & electric with the thousand nuances of hungry Life,
here we are & here we'll always be, alone but never separate,
lost but always found, here in our fingertips you'll always find me,
breathless & alive, waiting & always willing,
for the moment, for the Moonlight, for the secrets & the lust,
just let me watch you, just a moment, bathing in nothing but the Starlight,
this is it, the purpose & the grand finale, this is it,
the profound intensity of these
sweet & simple things...

LOVE AMONG THE NOMADS

Just take
that highway
& go, just smile & take
that journey, just shake it all off,
the small town, the small town dreams,
just take that airstream trailer,
that jeep, that highway leading who knows
where but always to the future,
just take your dreams & unfold them
each toward their mysterious paths within
your Life, just smile, just get up & break all those
old & tiresome mirrors, tomorrow's mirrors
are the rivers & the lakes & the great rolling blue
thunder of the skies, just kiss tomorrow goodbye
as easily as you shake off yesterday's dust, just live in the ecstasy
of the moment & feel the fragrant wind of the galaxies
sweeping through the glorious golden crown of your sunlit hair,
just pull on your jeans, lace up your boots & tilt back
your wide brimmed hat, just hit that petal & go,
like the first & last of the glorious nomads who let go lightly,
but hang on tightly to each of our daily miracles,
you are the future unbound & the freedom I see in each
raging of the waves & each subtle shiver of the Moonlight,
be everything we could have been & more,
I & the thousand other Lovers who embraced but a moment
in the rainbows & lost our innocence somewhere in the constellations,
just be beautiful, bright & loving, just forget whoever
you were & why, just discover everything
you might yet be...

A STRANGE & WONDROUS MAGIC

Perhaps
it's all over,
& I'll just walk away,
perhaps it's all over, just dust
& memories not yet faded,
this won't be the first time nor the last,
perhaps it's all done with, like a house of sensual cards,
fragrant with old blossoms & now scattering
to the twilight, perhaps the west wind calls & my ship
lies waiting in the harbour, a thousand times I've dreamed
of taking that voyage, of embracing danger yet again
on the wild fringes of unknown constellations,
perhaps it's for the best or at least inevitable, the human story
is always the same & always too quickly ended, except
among the truly quick, alive & brave, the human dance
is merciless & the Cosmos is compassionate but always fair,
I wanted you it's true, but I think I wanted something deeper,
kinder & more generous, I wanted you to be everything I could never be
& that's how foolish the Heart is, how relentlessly human I actually was,
I wanted a goddess even though I was at best a holy fool,
perhaps tomorrow will forgive us, in all its unknown prophecies
& miracles, but I doubt it, I think kisses will always be kisses
& dreams will always be dreams, eternity after eternity,
so long as heartbeats yearn & Magic mixes
a strange & wondrous spell...

ALL TRUE WILD THINGS

I might
have died here,
alone & adrift in the roses,
I might have died here,
like all true wild things do in the end,
I might have died here, unknown & unmourned,
except for the wildflowers pressed lightly
for a moment by the dust of my golden bones,
I might have died here, never caring,
except for the sunlight warm upon my dust
& the wind gently wafting me to the seasons,
I might have died here & perhaps I did, to bloom again
in far future Beauty, I might have died here but today
the Cosmos had different plans & who am I to question them,
especially since this is what I was born for,
this Magic, this miracle, this tragedy so essential to the rainbows,
I never belonged yet I was never gone, like a pilgrim
just smiling & passing through, tonight's the night
when the Earth turns & all things are possible,
tonight I come fearless, tonight I lay the bright burning sword
between each silence of your heartbeats,
this might have been tomorrow or it might have been yesterday,
in this blooming bright human garden, I came
because I somehow had to, because there's a thousand unlike me,
pallid & aflame with lesser blooms, I came because here
on these wild mountains sacred to the Moonlight never will I wither,
I am who I must be & I serve a mighty river, I serve
the constellations who dance amid us, I never care the reason,
I destroy & I create, I survive because the sky needs me

& the strange whispers in my soul, I survive because tonight is alive
& all flowers go down gently, into dreams
except this one...

THE RAINBOWS OR THE GLORY

I'm not
who I was,
& I never will be again,
I'm not who I once was,
but none of us are, not really,
in the deep confessional infinities
between each heartbeat & the next,
I'm not who I was, no knight, no hero, no rogue,
no rascal, & no bright & shining Lover,
I'm not whoever you once dreamed I'd be,
I'm just this simple man with these simple hands,
I'm just this child grown impossibly old,
I'm just this magician sadly lacking in wisdom but wise
beyond my years in a conjurer's complex imaginings,
some days it's like I was never here at all & all this carnage
was nothing but the dangerous ripples of untamed waters,
I'm not who I was & who you once danced with,
I'm not who you kissed, who you embraced lithe & naked
beneath the Moon, I'm just someone who saw the path & took it,
I'm just someone the Cosmos loved, I'm just a season the Earth
always brought forth & unfolded into blossoms, I'm just a leaf, bruised
& battered & scarlet stained, open hearted & aching, gently
rocking in the arms of the divine & most precious Mother of us all,
all I ask is a moment, a sigh, a wisp of enduring comfort,
each morning rises & the universe unfolds, eternal as yesterday
& tomorrow both beckoning, I'll ride on, I'll still conquer
in each battle allotted me, even in this, my last & my greatest,
this darkness bears a smiling face & I almost love it,
no matter the storm it brings, no matter
the rainbows or the glory...

41

GENTLE TO ME, DANCING

I always
knew you'd come,
gentle to me dancing,
I always knew you'd come,
like the soft hush of twilight when all
secrets unravel & the Cosmos spreads wide
its great shining arms of redemption,
I always knew you'd come, a thousand times,
when I lay bleeding, when my Heart was too human
& torn to the far flung dangers of this mysterious world,
I always knew my battlefields were your sacred ground,
your perfect burials of all imperfect dreams,
I always knew I needed nothing more than the soft electric
ecstasy of your kiss, each time it raised me & brought me home,
loving, ghostly & promised everything, of all things
I know only you are holy, only you are true,
only you are the Rapture & the miracle of the flesh,
each atom that revives me shimmers with your whisper,
I see the great sweep of the horizons & the trembling of each
new found blossom, my halo was broken & shot full of holes,
long ago & far away, my halo was broken & cast willingly to
the amorous waves & wind, whoever I am I know that I'm unworthy,
I know I'm the least of your Lovers except that you touch me
with the tenderness of yesterday's long healed disasters,
just lie with me here, like you always do, like you always intended to,
just lie with me & embrace me, like the shiver of Moonlight,
like the tentative miracle of each morning, like the sunlight, like the flash
of Beauty breaking across the waves, I know the words but only

42

yesterdays & the fleeting scent of forsaken orchards still need them,
you're here & that's all that matters, you're here
& I finally know the secret...

JUST ASK THE RAVENS

I'm
just here,
witnessing & waiting,
slowly dancing, slowly learning,
slowly redeeming myself
in the sunlight & the rain, who I was
can barely be remembered, & only
tomorrow knows the Magic the dawn brings forth,
I'm just here, perhaps for a simple heartbeat,
perhaps for each infinity of your dreams,
all I know I lost somewhere in the Rainbows,
somewhere in the Light that renders all wisdom useless,
just ask the ravens & you will find me,
among the wild things grown suddenly thoughtful,
as if silence was sensuous & delightful,
once you heard me at your window & whispering
in the leaves, Come out, Come out, I'd always say, Come out
& kiss the starlight, feel the Cosmos on your skin,
come out shyly & embrace me, knowing I'll always need you,
knowing I'll always love you in my strange & savage way,
once you heard me & then you lost me & then the Magic went away,
as if the season shifted & wild white phantoms
hunted in the snow, once you lost me & never even came looking,
at least not sincerely & never for long, once you almost caught me
but I was free & fierce & fleet of foot, once I was a Hero
& you were a precious maiden, but that was long ago
& the constellations can't remember, except
on mystic nights like this one, when Magic truly lives
& all lost Lovers are somehow
found...

44

A HINT OF FLOWERS DANCING

My Heart
was broken,
a thousand gentle times
like sunlight scattering
across the deep & mystic waters,
my Heart was broken, as if ravaged
by the Moonlight, as if taken
by the swift silver deer of shimmering Beauty,
my Heart was torn each time the dawn
touched me & there you were, still sleeping
lightly on my shoulder, as if your each exquisite breath
was a miracle I was barely worthy of,
just take me now to that strange & subtle Rapture
that exists so delicate in our fingertips,
to that endless ecstasy of the Sky where all Love
is finally possible, amid the long lost Stars & the profusion
of the Rainbows, just lead me, guide me,
touch me in each of those sweet sensual Mysteries
where the Earth turns & comes to know itself, just reach me
in these far flung nebulae still drifting amid our atoms,
for my gift I bring you silence & the serene slowness of my Spirit
unfolding, gently into blossom, I bring you this moment,
empty handed but with every unknown river of my nature finally
flowing homeward, to you & the Cosmos in your eyes,
let these constellations shimmer & finally enfold us,
my Heart was broken, finally into this infinity, so that only you
could lightly enter, almost unnoticed at first,
like the first faint whisper of Spring,
& the hint of flowers
dancing...

EACH HALO OF SHOOTING STARS

Just kiss me
& save me,
that's all I care about,
all I need, all I long for,
just embrace me as if quietly cradling
my weary & war torn Heart,
as if my Spirit had been given over
into your keeping, just grant me your miracle,
your Mercy that is truly immaculate & boundless,
just reach me, somewhere across these wild
& dangerous waves, these storms, these tempests
that swept me up with a hungry exhilaration that almost
lost me forever these fair & fragrant shores,
I was what I was & I went forth bravely,
my furrow was fierce, free & scarlet through
the golden bladed meadows of this world, I knew
everything was Beautiful but beauty is an exquisite & fleeting
electricity sacred to the heartbeat, the fire within the eyes
that so resembles the constellations, all is Holy with me now,
all is true, all is pure, in the deepest & most human way,
I was here & still I almost linger, so long as our lips
are compassionate & this night is long, all things change,
evolve & grow, all dreams set fire the nebulae dancing,
I don't know you & I probably never will, except I see the Cosmos
shining, shyly & in the first faint blush of innocence
in the tenderness of your Eyes, your hair is silver with each halo
of the shooting Stars, we're here but a moment, but a heartbeat
infinite with all possibilities, whatever tomorrow brings I hear it

in your whispers, amorous with anticipation,
whatever I know of Ecstasy I feel it in the light lingering
butterflies of your fingertips...

A TASTE OF THE MOON

I'll just
kiss you once,
I'll just kiss you once
& then I'll turn away, fleeting
as the twilight but immortal
as the Moon, I'll just kiss you once
but it will taste like infinity,
like the Cosmos condensed to a brief
mingling of lips & sensual tongues,
I'll just kiss you once but there'll be a lifetime in it,
a dance of shadows, delight & Rapture,
I'll just kiss you once, because to kiss you twice
would stop the world, the Earth might shiver with delight
& dangerous tides might rise, mountains might even
crumble & the constellations shine in immense
& miraculous new Magics, I'll just kiss you once
& then slowly leave, because even the slightest flicker
of your fingertips across my chest might break me, might
bend me in impossible postures, as if a dancer consumed by
exquisite new rhythms, just tell me all you ache for,
in the faint fragrance of your hair rippling across my shoulders,
Eternity should come like this, as a Mystery to be tasted,
touched & savoured, words are useless, and as meaningless as
hopes, fears or dreams, we're here & the Cosmos loves us, here, now
& forever, for a heartbeat we're divine & that's always enough,
here in the Rainbows & the trembling of each blossom born to Beauty,
here in the sunlight & the hint of sensual summers,
here in the Light that suddenly reveals us,
naked but never alone...

NIGHTFALL

I was
lonely
but I was brave,
at least sometimes,
I was lonely but I had
a thousand Lovers, a thousand
moonlit nights softly shimmering
with the delight of new found kisses,
I was lonely but that never stopped me,
that never kept me from the sunlight
so exquisite sometimes in my Heart,
I was lonely but I was brave & I fought each
battle of the Spirit, each hopeless but windswept miracle
of the rainbows, I was lonely but it never mattered,
I just used each tear to nurture each subtle greening of the Earth,
each tremulous blossom newborn & aching for fulfillment,
I was brave, broken, & born again into each newfound Cosmos,
into each great coming forth of the Light across the sensual stirring
of the oceans, I just sought you through each season,
each sandstorm, each storm seeming so savage & determined
to rip the Stars, I just stayed here dancing, sometimes lithe,
sometimes graceful, but sometimes like some strange eagle
with both wings broken, I knew you were coming,
I knew you were Beautiful & that's all that really mattered,
that's all I truly lived for, that final moment of truth & Rapture
when our atoms intermingled, I don't care where you are, not tonight at least
& perhaps never again in this subtle infinity of the flesh,
I don't even care if you remember, because I finally see you everywhere,
just like you always intended, I always hear your whisper

& I know you're always with me,
if not tomorrow then at least in this endless
mystery of the nightfall...

YOUR EVERY HEARTBEAT

Just
always Love me,
that's all I ask & all I
dream of, just always love me,
even when our bones crumble,
even when our dreams dissolve to golden dust,
just always love me, somehow, somewhere,
as long as it's forever, as long as we linger,
even faintly amid the constellations,
even but a moment in the exquisite trembling
of the dewdrops, let no wave be too wild, nor sorrow
ever too deep to separate us, let us forget
about tomorrow & the uncertain eyes of future Lovers,
each breath is forever, even in the moment of its passing,
even in the fleeting frenzy of all fingertips, just never leave me,
just redeem me, just release me to the Stars in the sure
& sensuous certainty of your embrace, just forgive me
my thousand transgressions, my vanities, my ridiculous braveries
& the willful blindness of my eyes, just accept me as this fool,
this human, this wild & frenzied thing from each magic forest of the Earth,
whatever I was I could have been better, I could have been kinder, gentler,
more conscious of time's sands so slipping through my fingers,
just kiss me & let that be all we say forever except in the Cosmos
of our dreams, I was your handsome man & you were my brown eyed Beauty,
each dawn when dawn still shone, when limbs were nimble
& smiles were quick, it's the journey in the end that matters,
never the unknown goal or destination, it's the journey & the companion
who never leaves you, it's the once & future maiden who becomes
the miracle, it's the embrace of the tender Spirit who
savours your every heartbeat...

51

A ROSE, REMEMBERED

You were

the Rose who

always bloomed, somewhere

in my Heart, somewhere

in my Spirit when the north winds blew

& my every atom shivered,

you were the river who always cleansed me,

who always embraced me, subtle

in the sensual intensity of each Midnight,

now long lost in each desolate landscape of my memories,

I met an intensity of rainbows, unasked for but impossible

to resist, I met an intensity of rainbows, & a cascade

of emotions that swept away our world, the Stars seemed

too bright & always cruelly calling, I told you I loved you,

with every profound truth still rooted in my innocence

& that's all I cling to now, when nothing means anything,

except the relentless sifting of fleeing galaxies through my fingers,

I no longer count the years but only the heartbeats,

the heartfelt intensities I've spent without you, you were the Rose

who always bloomed & our garden was the one sweet gift

I was given in this world, I see you even now, down by the riverside,

up in the meadows of the summer mountains, I remember the taste of you,

& the simple flavours still so unknown then but always

promising everything, I know the twilight loved us & perhaps

even the Cosmos, when at last I knew that our bones were holy

& the miracles of our bodies & our dreams, I knew the world began then

& the Rapture haunts me still, when your touch was

exquisite with anticipation & I forgot everything,
except our constellations
aching to explode...

A KISS OF SUNFLOWERS

Nights

are always

the hardest, when the Moon

calls me, so amorous, sweet & free,

Nights are always the hardest,

the deepest, the truest, Mystery always

haunts me & whispers in the fleeting voices

of fading Lovers, I lie down but my dreams keep dancing,

I stare out the windows & there we are again,

up in the high summer meadows, there we are,

a thousand years ago & yet almost safe in the embrace

of tomorrow, sometimes I think you're here to help me,

to redeem me at least until the dawn slyly smiles,

I can't do it on my own, you know that, I can't resist you

nor the subtle irresistible urging of the nebulae, sometimes I'm scared,

but sometimes my Spirit just breaks free of this temporary cage

of flesh & blood & bone, sometimes I'm there again, brave

& raging at the comets, brave & leading yet another charge

across all the futile battlefields of my life, sometimes I'm there again,

man, myth & monster, open to everything, still believing, still staggering,

still wounded but wondrous with my bright blue pilgrim eyes,

all things return, all seasons, all rivers, all exquisite raptures

of newborn breath, I'll live today & I'll fly tomorrow, that's the way it is

& the way it always will be, I've seen the writing on the wall except

it was carved upon an oak tree, long ago & far away, it said kiss me forever,

each moment you come closer, each moment you almost feel the rapture,

young hearts will live forever, no matter the storm, wild wind or dark water, young Hearts will live, innocent & profound, in fields as endless as the sunlight, like a kiss of sunflowers or the taste of subtle honey, so soothing to the tongue...

AMID THE NAKED & THE NEBULAE

I crossed
my swords, beneath
the starlight on the mountain,
I crossed my swords & came down into your valley,
expecting nothing, just tired beyond all possible
meanings of the word, just aching, in Heart & broken Spirit,
I just crossed my swords & hoped for redemption,
somewhere amid the simple fields & the gentle sunrise,
I just hoped for connection to whatever was within me
that might still possibly be called human, I just came home,
in some strange & innocent moment, as if childhood
was just an interrupted journey & all dreams might begin again,
I just came into your valley, set like an ancient jewel beneath
the blue ridges of the mountains, I came seeking you, before I even
knew your name, before I even guessed that Love was still yet possible,
I waited in the cornfields, in the tall grasses, in the groves
of amorous whispers, I waited until I finally saw you & emerged
a simple man, holy in the humble honesty of my intentions,
I came forward & honoured each of your customs, each of your beliefs
& each of the mysterious magics of your constellations,
I believed in you & that's all that really mattered, I lived from dawn to dawn
& breath to breath, I lived until the mad gods came & storms
raised the thunder of the constellations, I lived until each kiss
became our last one & I heard the great bronze horn upon the skyline,
I went forth proud, again to the savage flare of galaxies, I took up
my armour & there I was again, amid the cannon fire of the comets,
here I am unless your fingertips can at last reach me, out here
where death & life are almost one, out here where you must seek me,

at the cost of everything you own, out here where each of us
is somehow beautiful, amid the naked & the newborn
smiles of nebulae...

WHERE THE WOLVES ARE SILENT

Just
rock me now,
gently now & with no hope
of tomorrow, just rock me now, just let me rest,
at least a moment, in hope of sweeter dreams,
in hope of Dawn rising yet once more,
just rock me, just redeem me, just reach back,
through the disasters & perilous voyages,
just see me, again as the brave young man who loved you,
just see me laughing, blue eyed, wild haired,
powerful & graceful with each miracle of the moment,
just hold me & let me drift into the graceful constellations
always shimmering in your eyes, just be with me, here in this last night
where everything is possible, just embrace me with the tenderness of oceans,
with the infinity of subtle galaxies, just let my heartbeat rest, as gentle
as a child, in this ending of all rainbows, this dance so slow & sensual
& infinite in its Rapture, I wonder where the galaxies are, I wonder
& then I know, they're right here within us, in this Cosmos that never sleeps,
in this glow, this Love, this Ecstasy of flesh & blood & bone so
slowly fading into the Stars, perhaps tomorrow comes, either here
or on yet another of the far flung worlds, perhaps I'll find the whispers
to finally say goodbye to every madness that ever haunted me, you're all
I ever wanted, truly & forever, you're all I ever wanted & with each
faltering of my heartbeat I realize it even more, I realize the Mystery of it,
with each healing halo of your fingertips, our skin may fail us,
& our muscles & our minds, we may fail & just scatter like dust,
forlorn to the great conflagration of the atoms, we may fail but never
our Spirits, never each breath we shared, so fierce & yet so fleeting,

never our Spirits & they shine forever, out where the wolves are silent
& nothing is ever promised, except a Kiss
that lasts forever...

SOMETIMES, THE STARS ARE MY LOVERS

Sometimes
the Stars are my Lovers,
but most often they are my mentors,
my teachers, my beacons
that keep me going, that keep me riding
each wild horse of my imagination,
sometimes the Stars just smile slyly & pretend
they know the Cosmos, sometimes they lead me onward
& teach me the strange magic of their glory,
sometimes they teach me courage, endurance, empathy,
sometimes they whisper & take me dancing,
out amid the brightest & most beauteous of the earthly angels,
the shimmering maidens who bloom but a moment
in each of the immortal summers, I have lost myself, gladly,
in the eyes of each sensual Midnight, in the fragrance of youth
& the supple grace of an exquisite body willingly offered,
some people envy me, but that's just because they don't truly
understand the Rainbows, the true & rugged Beauty behind each miracle,
you think we're here to laugh, but that's only partly true,
you think we're here to weep, but that's just a fleeting heartbeat,
we're here because nothing else truly matters, no Dawn ever truly rises
except for the blue rapture of the sky or the perfect cleansing tears of rain,
you think that I want you but that's just because you're brave
& see our Hearts carved upon Life's great Tree,
I've slept almost forever down deep in the enduring arms
of the amorous Earth where all bones & blood & dreams are born,
I've been everything, & everything is always new,
everything is always reborn, like a river always flowing
& a prophecy of Bliss...

SOMETIMES, IN STRANGE WHISPERS

You can
almost hear me,
sometimes, just beneath
the whispering of the leaves,
you can almost hear me & see me & touch me,
at least a moment, in each sensuous
mystery of the Midnight, you know who I am
& why I come to you so slyly, so sweetly, so subtly loving,
you know who I am but as yet you cannot name me,
you cannot conjure me except by the magic
of the Moonlight that dances even in the day,
you think I'm laughing, but in truth I'm sighing,
I'm trembling in the Grace of you, in the Serenity, in the Light,
I've crossed a thousand oceans & known the exquisite
sighs of summer maidens, I've known each ecstasy
our breath so fleetingly grants us, the dawn may rise but somehow
I see it only in your eyes, you touch me & transform me,
from everything I am into everything I yet might be,
you're the enigma of each heartbeat, unknown even to yourself
though the Cosmos stirs within you, it's impossible you should Love me
& yet the rivers flow & the seasons shine & the nebulae draw us deeper,
where we'll go to I can't even begin to imagine,
our fate just shimmers electric in the fingers of each galaxy,
in the complex flavours of each kiss, I know the dance you long for,
the flicker of fingertips that make you ache, I know
you're the new world rising, & the joyous trembling of the waters,
I know all miracles redeem us & our flesh kindles a thousand Stars,
I know tomorrow is a long time & each rapture is uncertain,

I know we're promised nothing, but you make me brave
& that almost makes me holy, you make me vulnerable
& that almost makes me
Pure...

A SONG FOR ALL BRAVE LOVERS

Sometimes
I was lonely,
sometimes I was nothing
but a kite forsaken in strange
storms beneath the Moon, sometimes
I was a Spirit forbidden,
like lost Light breaking across the waters,
sometimes I was the dancer
you always dreamed of, even when you feared me,
even when I whispered outside your midnight window,
naked in the mystery of erotic constellations,
sometimes I was the Hero you somehow conjured
to shatter the temples that enslaved you, sometimes I was
your Lover & sometimes I was your guide,
in each sensual upheaval of a wild & windswept Cosmos,
sometimes we sailed together, arm in arm toward
exotic & unknown horizons, sometimes we embraced
& our galaxies mingled in a great conflagration of our atoms,
sometimes each kiss was electric with the comets, breaking across
the mountains & descending into flames amid the festivals of the flesh,
sometimes we were simple, chaste, & almost childlike
in the eerie innocence of our twilights & the sleepy glories of our dawns,
sometimes I almost loved you with a strength that made
the Universe shatter, sometimes the sunlight sought us,
slowly dancing in the meadows, skin to skin & quietly delirious
in the erotic eternity of each heartbeat, sometimes we just held on,
in each shattering of our world, in each shaking of the leaves,
in each coming of the winter, in each departing of the sparrows,
sometimes we were nothing but flesh & blood & bone,
long departed & almost forgotten...

A SWEET SLOW DANCER

You're
the one Dream
I can't let go of, the simple
truth that somehow defines the world,
you're the Goddess, earthly but profound,
the Mystery of eyes & touch & skin
that slips so fleeting through my fingers,
I'm not this joker, this magician, this madman
who stands before you, I'm not the Poet who's embraced you
a thousand times beneath the amorous Moonlight,
I'm the strange ghost of yesterday who alone among the multitudes
bends his knee & truly sees you, wait a little longer
& I'll prove it in every exquisite & intriguing way
our flesh always falls heir to, I know you're dangerous,
proud & gifted in ways not even the galaxies comprehend,
I know you're a Mystery even to yourself but I'm a sweet slow dancer
& I kiss as if forever, the strength of the eons is within me,
the power, the pain & the crystal clarity of the dew, I'm coming for you
but you already know that, in each slow ecstasy of your breath,
when you search the mirror for the thousand miracles of youth,
& grace & magic, all mercy is within you & that alone will redeem me,
that alone will guide me, in these lost & golden days, beside
the waves of the sea where dragons rise, & all wisdom is fragrant
with galaxies, & the Cosmos smiles, here where your fingertips
gently guide me, like a child into the great merging of the rivers,
beneath the nebulae & the bliss
of endless Light...

UNTIL THE WILD STARS COME

I thought
I knew you,
& perhaps I did, at least
until the Mystery deepened,
at least until the wild Stars came out
& all promises were broken,
I thought I stood on firm ground,
on soil sacred to the Cosmos & the mystic dances
of the galaxies, I thought you knew me
& were serene, chaste, & a miracle warm & sensuous
in the Midnight, I thought I could tell you everything,
like a Goddess come to guide me, like a Muse,
like a maiden faithful through each of our eternal summers,
I thought you came with the Spring & embraced me
through each cool & crystalline winter, bone to bone
& root to root through the freezing & rebirth of the mystic soil
& shimmering flesh, I thought you were simple, open & profound,
graceful, abundant & merciful, I thought you were everything
I dreamed of, in each lost & lonely labyrinth of my Heart,
I thought you were Beautiful & that's the only true insight I had,
the only true gift bequeathed by the nebulae always aloft & watching,
serenely above each of our embraces, perhaps I was a joker, a fool,
a child in the Universe's great plan, but that was just because you loved me,
that was just because the sunlight caressed you & the wind
ravished your hair, lightly with fragrant fingers, that was just because
you believed in me while I was still a phantom of smoke & mirrors,
you laid it all down for me, each treasure, each trembling confession
& each key to your hidden valleys, you laid it all down
& I didn't see the dawn breaking across the waters,
I didn't see the rainbows & the simple rapture of each kiss,

just forgive me now & kiss me on my weathered brow,
I don't know you & I never will, at least not completely,
I don't know you & that will always redeem us,
until at last we transcend to Mercy,
you're the journey my Spirit always grapples with
& I'm the Magic you can't resist...

EACH EXQUISITE DREAM

Here I kneel,
in the Mystery, in the Magic,
in the promise of yet another
ecstatic breath, at least until the Cosmos
claims my bones & all dust to dust returns,
here I kneel, the knight, the poet, the charlatan,
here I kneel, deserving nothing perhaps but somehow
still expecting everything, here I kneel, hungry
but humbled by Grace & ever hopeful of your mercy,
here I kneel, here at the beginning of all things, here where
the Midnight whispers erotic imaginings to its paramour the Moon,
I know you now, & I see you in the rainbows of each
of my infinite disasters, I thought I'd seen the Light but that
was just the flickering of each brave & transient constellation,
it's you I love, you I worship, you I almost fear in case you should
ever leave me, you're so young & proud & open hearted, a shelter
from all storms, & a safe haven from all dangers, I feel you
in my bloodstream & the erotic textures of your breath bequeath
all earthly secrets when your lips pass like the flicker of butterflies
across my chest, just take me now, just use me, just raise me,
infinite into the cathedral of the nebulae, I know where I am now
& what my purpose is, I'm here & a thousand years ago, a million even,
back when a heartbeat was just a heartbeat, newly trembling from the void,
I know who you are at last, you're the lover, the laughter, the maiden
& the crone, you're the madonna as yet unrevealed, you're the quiet comfort
of Beauty sheer & never ceasing, you're the rapture always trembling,
just a moment before I reach it, you're the journey
that never ends & bequeaths
each exquisite dream...

IN THE BEAUTY OF YOUR WHISPERS

I knew
you were divine,
& mysterious & loving,
I knew you were loving, divine & beautiful,
I knew you were subtle with the Mystery
of each cell shimmering, with the inherent Magic
of each infinite breath that binds us to the Cosmos,
I knew you were my Lover, my guide, my journey
& each wild ocean I set my Heart to sail upon, I knew you were
Beauty, incarnate & yet exquisitely fleeting, I knew we were
bones open to the constellations, dancing today & dust tomorrow,
I knew our skin was our exquisite tapestry of earthly rainbows,
I knew Spring would always love us, winter would always howl
& all things would drift at last to the embrace of the amorous Stars,
I knew you loved me, even if you went among the blossoms
& took a thousand Lovers, I could see it in your eyes, I could taste it
in your kiss, each of our embraces subtly shook the world,
I knew you were the Muse come to haunt me, to electrify me
with the shimmering of your fingertips, I knew it all but as yet
understanding eluded me, I knew I was a child & always innocent
& vulnerable, I knew I was a child ancient in my anguish & still
somehow proud in my knight's bright armour, I was the hero you might have
dreamed of, back when dreams were simple & day danced so sharply
divided from the midnight, I know you embrace me, as if there was
no other nor ever could be, I know you just love me, love me, love me,
I know you have no choice & wouldn't have it any other way,
I know what we were born for & why we met, here at the crossroads
of all certainty, where decisions are made & regrets are useless,

just let me taste you, like an apple fit only for the gods,
just let me watch you & lose myself in the beauty
of your whispers...

AN ANCIENT HERO, REMEMBERING

Just
take me back
to where it all began,
just take me back to that gentle season,
to that first blooming of the blossoms,
just take me back, just redeem me, just remember me,
just take me back, to that deep green valley,
to that simple time & that long lost season,
just take me back to that cabin beside the river,
to those fields & ancient groves,
just let me believe & watch the harmony of the skies,
just let me dance with you, as chastely beneath the Moon
as if we had never been wild & tempestuous Lovers,
I'm a thousand miles away, a million even, & the Earth
seems shattered & the journey relentless & unceasing,
once I knew the oceans & each far shore seemed fair & fragrant,
now the cannon fire never ceases & dangerous ghosts ride
remorseless across the fields, I see you in each mirror the Stars
lay across the waters, I see you slowly brush your hair, the dark waves
soft & sensual in the Midnight, just let me rest my eyes upon you
& feel your exquisite whispers at least a moment in my ear,
just let my legs sustain me & let my Heart stay open, just let
my Spirit guide me, I listened to everyone but I should have believed
only you, I'm done with fear, bravery & every other proud delusion,
I'm done with everything that won me the battles but lost me
each of my eternal summers, the days are long
& I'll never rest again, unless at last
in the haven of your arms...

A GODDESS, IN THE MUSIC

Just
set me free,
just set me free to love you,
to worship you, to reveal you,
just set me free, for I see
all your lives within you, all your magics,
all your Beauties, all your dreams,
just set me free & forgive me, just set me free
& embrace me, in spite of my lust, my greed
& my thousand transgressions,
just set me free, for I come to you humbled & yet holy,
broken & yet proud, I want to touch you,
not like a young man but like a pure one,
I want to release you, to redeem you before you ever stray
from every sacred innocence the Moonlight sweetly bequeathed you,
I saw you & I was smitten, irrevocably, with the tide
of the Cosmos dancing, with the bright eyes of the nebulae
forever watching & waiting with baited breath,
I saw the Sunlight lingering, for that one exquisite moment in your hair
that suddenly revealed the world, I know you're the one
great gift the Universe always allows all true & faithful poets,
you're young & beautiful & proud, but in the end that's just the journey,
the gradual opening of your eyes so the galaxies dwell
within them, I've seen you a thousand times & the first faint miracle
of daylight always lingered on our lips when we rose & went
our separate ways, all wanderers return at last to the birthplace
where true souls meet, I heard you in the music
& I suddenly knew who you were, I heard you
in the music always aching
to be played...

71

A FINAL WHISPER OF THE DAWN

Perhaps
I'll meet you in the garden,
perhaps I'll meet you,
when all this fire & fury is done,
perhaps I'll meet you, at least for a moment
when we lay our burdens down,
perhaps I'll meet you & even kiss you,
with the final full truth of my heartbeat,
perhaps I'll forget & just embrace the moment,
innocent & as wonder filled as the child I probably never was,
perhaps all Dreams will linger & all kisses tingle
with youth, innocence & the promise of eternal summers,
perhaps it'll all have some sort of meaning, some fleeting promise
of eternity & the strange sly rapture of the Stars,
perhaps I'll break these chains & forget these shadows,
no warfare lasts forever, no anger lingers, nor hatred, lust or envy,
no anger lingers when the last bell shakes the valley,
when the tremors shimmer like the rising of the Wave,
I see you & I see you now, in the Garden, in the shining sweet fingers
of this earthly paradise, I finally see you, here in this last
naked confession of my Spirit as the storm of wings grows subtle
but softly imminent, I was what I was & what I never was,
it's easy to blame everyone else but at the end I must embrace
each wild highway that somehow bewitched me, I was nothing but a knight
in a fool's bright armour, just embrace me, just hold me, just redeem me,
we're here at this crossroad, in this last & most fiery & fatal moment,
we're here & all past promises are useless, either we hang on or we
lose it all, either we dare to love & seek each new world together, or we fall,

either we touch & finally believe in each other, or the night wind seeks us
& Light finally forsakes the trembling of the waves
& the one final whisper of the Dawn...

A SMALL BIRD SHINING

I heard
a small bird calling,
so lightly it might have been
my conscience, I heard a small bird
calling & I suddenly knew
I had to Love you or regret it forever,
I knew I had to believe,
I had to be courageous, foolhardy & forgiving,
I heard a small bird calling, somewhere in this dawn
of all redemption & infinite promise,
I knew I had to rise, & kneel & rise again,
I knew I had to reel into darkness & somehow still
lead you toward the Light, a small bird called & all things
became possible, I knew I had to accept you, exactly as you were,
complex upon the cross of divided loyalties & cruel
with the wounds of innocence & ecstasy dancing so close together,
a small bird called & I suddenly remembered who I was
& what I was here for, I suddenly remembered why the Cosmos
chose me from a thousand hearts more virtuous & deserving,
I suddenly knew & the price I had to pay, I suddenly knew all I had to do
was believe, to open myself to Beauty & the truth of each erotic fingertip,
I knew we all lie down naked at the end & all else is misplaced vanity,
let the flowers come to me, the wild groves, the Dreams,
the exquisite sunsets, truly I am infinite but only in your eyes,
only if at last I finally reveal you, golden in that sunlit miracle when
youth reclaims the universe, when darkness rests awhile & we small quick
creatures dance across this earthly constellation, I'm always here for you now,

I know what my purpose is, our dust will shine, perhaps
but a moment, but the world will remember you, I swear it,
with every Grace somehow given
into my hands...

SARAH SAILS AWAY

I just
knew you,
for a moment before
the leaves fell, I just knew you
& I rested a moment in your Beauty,
I just knew you & for a moment I knew all things,
I felt the Cosmos, the heartbeat,
the heartache all Lovers fall prey to in the end,
you're so close I can almost touch you,
so fragrant, so aching & exquisite in the moment,
I just knew you & now you might almost be leaving,
at least there's a ship waiting in the harbour,
a sensual tide already promised to the Moonlight,
perhaps time & kisses, & fleeting erotic touches have no
enduring meaning, in fact in the end I almost believe it must be so,
I was the most inconstant of your Lovers, just as you
were the most mysterious of mine, I never knew
what you were thinking nor where your passions led you,
you said I was almost magic, a dream cool & exquisite
sliding through the prosaic gardens of your life, perhaps that's true,
but you were the small & gentle miracle of each of my mornings,
I never quite caught the whirlwind of your wings when you danced
among the rainbows, I was ancient & exotic with a thousand disasters
& yet I was innocent in your eyes, you called me young & perhaps
I almost believed you, perhaps I already realized your eyes
would always haunt me, no matter which shore we finally lay upon,
either embracing or just a pyre of windswept bones, perhaps I just knew you,
& knew the Cosmos loved us, at least for the eternity that always
lingered when the Universe guided us, gently but firmly,
into the ecstasy of our arms...

76

DANGEROUS DREAMS

Perhaps
you broke my Heart,
or perhaps I broke it myself
& just handed you the pieces,
perhaps I behaved unwisely & you had
intentions Beautiful & profound,
we placed such value on this single trembling
of our heartbeats, we both loved, without ever
meaning to but wildly & with complete abandon,
why I said what I said I'll never know,
except I was tired & exhausted from my previous journeys
& mesmerized by you, I knew you were
a sensual gift of the Cosmos, ecstatic in every limb,
I knew you were young, impatient & proud, I knew you
meant well but were uncertain & swept away by an unknown river,
I should have known better but I always heard the music
of the wind, the sea & the rain, I knew I was so ancient
I saw a different world, you created a palace that all amorous daydreams
drifted toward, at least for the exquisite infinity of a heartbeat,
who you are & who I am I no longer have any clear idea,
I no longer know if the dawn will ever rise again, except that
I know it will because our path is the never ending path of the poet
unto the goddess, I've kissed a thousand maidens
but in the end I know there's truly only you, so subtle
& shining with inner Grace, I know there's only you,
at least for this rising of the constellations
& this horizon of dangerous dreams...

AN AURA OF ANGELS

I was
just sitting there,
watching the river,
I was just sitting there & suddenly
I saw you, suddenly you were there,
mere moments before the Moonlight swept us away,
I was just sitting there, lost in an infinitude
of worlds & random constellations, I was just
sitting there, about to let it all go & just drift nameless
amid the nebulae, as if in the subtle rapture
of the last & most secret hallelujah, I was just there
& there you were, suddenly beside me & with galaxies
in your eyes, there you were when I thought yet another dream
had been broken & the midnight was edging in,
there you were, as exotic as the exquisite simplicity of a heartbeat,
as miraculous & mysterious as the innocence
of some wild & fragile creature, I knew you were my lover,
so sweet & breathless with the aura of imminent angels,
I couldn't have predicted you but before I knew it we were dancing,
naked in the open aching of our Spirits so akin to rainbows,
we were there, & that was the electricity of the touch the Earth finally
turned upon, now nothing is as it was & the waves
still ripple against the shoreline, where youth & ancient wisdom mingle
in the subtle mating of our atoms, this is the great gift,
the miracle never bestowed lightly but always to greater purpose,
you told me everything & I answered every whisper,
as if dreams had finally come to test me & today I became
everything I could have been & was born into that
new beginning always granted by erotic fingertips,
to mystics, knights & fools...

78

A SHIVERING OF THE MOON

I lost
myself because
I believed in you,
because I sought you out,
in wild & dangerous places,
I lost myself because I was innocence
& wisdom adrift on a windswept river,
who could have predicted you,
who could have been ready for that,
for the intense blue oceans of your eyes,
for the glories of sunlight dancing in your hair,
I lost myself & became something deeper, richer & wiser,
Magic was poring out of me & this simple world was shaken,
there was no beginning & no end to the journey we embarked upon,
the rapture & the subtle sublime bliss so softly spoken,
I lost myself & was broken & reborn & just wanted to heal you
with the erotic trembling of my fingers, I was lost
& my disasters were legendary, relentless in their reckless abandon,
I was lost but I drowned myself in you, I breathed you in
& saw as you saw & dreamed as you dreamed, I drew you in
& you shone like Light around me, in each of your infinite lives I loved you,
in each miraculous meadow of your sweet scented summers,
you were immortal, infinite & exquisite with atoms, I lost myself
& here I am, dishevelled, bewildered & smiling like a madman,
a gentle fool sitting beside you or lost in the beauty
of your breathing, watching the river beside you,
sometimes together, sometimes lost
in the shivering of the Moon...

LEAD ME HOMEWARD, ANGEL

I've loved you,
a thousand times,
a million even, age after age,
constellation after constellation,
I've loved you, worshipped you,
I've forsaken you, forgotten you & then been
brought low, like all heroes at the end,
I've been broken & brought low, in some dusty
desert town or some windswept meadow beneath the Stars,
I've loved you, loved you, loved you & that's been my purpose in life,
my meaning & the source of all magic that sustained me,
you are my rock, my gentle kingdom in each sensual mystery
of midnight after midnight, you are my rock, my temple,
my fierce fire burning when my enemies surround me,
this silence always seems so sacred when I finally remember
& there you are, lithe & shyly smiling, forever young by ancient rivers
& drawing cleansing water from the shining well all pilgrims
ache at the end to sip from, you are so fierce, so true, so sharp as a blade
& so cleansing as a blossom, all these wars I've fought, all these battles,
all these pointless victories, in the end they all mean nothing,
they are dust & the faint flickering tatters of forgotten pride,
we were the first ones, the Lovers, the simple rapture of each fleeting
Heartbeat, I know who I am now, & that is fierce & terrible
& also as subtle as the rain, I speak for no one now, except the Cosmos,
who first brought us forth, in infinite grace & mercy,
& the promise of Spring, always rising in each simple garden
exquisite beside all paths that somehow in the end
just lead us homeward...

WHERE OLD GHOSTS GO

Just
remember me,
because I'm still here dancing,
still here dreaming,
still here dying & being reborn,
just remember me, at least a moment,
in the Moonlight, in the mist so fleeting
across the waters, just remember how far I rode,
how far I came, just remember how high I climbed,
just to whisper to the rainbows,
just remember me, still golden by the water,
watching the sunlight linger in your hair,
yesterday came too quickly but the midnights
were always slow & sweet, at least I was the poet
you couldn't have dreamed of, the Lover who shook Life's
deepest & most sensual tree, I'm gone where old ghosts go now,
into the hills with a thousand echoes, into the windswept meadows,
into the wildwood where passion still sometimes lingers,
we shone in a single season & then drifted away in the scattering
of earthly leaves, the Moon is always rising, sweet & silver
across the endless waters, I'll just sail on, forgetting nothing
but aching for the Cosmos, remember me a moment,
at last as if you loved me, at least in that windswept moment,
when a touch was still electric, & our kiss
could define the world...

PARADISE

Paradise
is so near
it almost eludes me,
subtle & electric in your fingertips,
Paradise is so near & eternity
so fragile, as if fragrant but a moment on your lips,
I searched so long, & I journeyed so far,
as if each heartbeat was a blessing, as if each breath
was a miracle, Paradise is so near, as if invisible
but barely behind this weary earthly shell, I see you everywhere,
as if the Goddess in your eyes shines at last amid
this intangible conflagration of the constellations, Paradise is near,
& the sacred perfection of consummation blessed at last
by the Cosmos & the last & greatest Star, I know you'll never believe me,
not for a moment & not for an eternity, in this costume we're
always forced to wear, I cast myself upon the rough wild sea,
as if my bones, blood & yearning for Beauty had become at last immortal,
I believed all things but at last I believed in only you,
young, proud & defiant, golden haired & enigmatic in the prosaic
certainties of this fleeting world, I know you believed, at least a moment,
in every tale I told you while I searched so vainly for the truth,
I apologize but only briefly, here as the last Wave rises,
I should have been surer, quicker & braver in my prophecies,
I thought I had forever, but now I know the river flows with a purpose
all its own, I know I have you but could lose you forever, in those blue green
oceans of your eyes, I know you either believe me or lie down
beside me, in that sleep all Lovers endure,
when lost & cast astray...

A HERO, JUST TO LOVE YOU

Just let me
come home,
a moment in your arms,
just let me come home, this first
& last time only, just let me come home,
just as I always dreamed it, gentle
across the abyss that separates the subtle ecstasies
of our heartbeats, I guess a thousand years
was too long & yet too short for the cosmic dice to roll,
finally in our favour, I guess tomorrow is still smiling
& gently shaking yet another of summer's blossom clad branches,
I guess the wars still rage & the Stars still hang in the balance,
I guess the Earth still needs its heroes, its unwitting sacrifices
& naked pawns, to have found you & then have lost you, yet again,
over & over, is nothing short of ridiculous & yet the river still flows onward,
bright & miraculous with constellations & the quick bright shimmering
of lover's kisses, I just wanted you, even here in this peaceful valley
where I knew innocence was infinite & fragile as the last fleeting
& exquisite embrace of each miraculous breath, you're here & I'm here,
& the ancient gods laugh to see us still so hopeful & wondrous in our touch,
nothing is free here, except everything is but you're got to know the rules,
you've got to touch as if your Heart depended on it, you've got to kiss
as if memory had no meaning & the great wave was always rising,
as if to sweep away each pretence of solid ground, you've got to remember
what we always forget, that you are tall & proud & beautiful,
& I was fair & miraculous once myself, but became
a hero just to love you...

LOVE, AMID THE WILD FLOWERS

I'm
walking on,
sometimes laughing,
sometimes dancing, I'm walking on,
not because I want to but because
the river calls me & the Stars shimmer
with the fleeting ecstasy of yesterday's dreams,
I'm walking on, I'm sailing the rough
& uncharted waters yet again, I'm taking the voyage
when my boots lead me resolutely to the water,
the sails are set, the paddles are raised & once again
tomorrow's nothing but a promise & a whisper, I'm sailing on,
still breathing the exquisite air & feeling midnight's kiss
upon my brow, I wanted you, at least for a thousand years,
but it seems like we've already embraced in those ancient
wildflower meadows where Magic was alive & wild
with amorous eyes, it seems no one loves a prophet unless
he speaks with a golden tongue, it seems no one wants a poet
except when passion smiles & sweeps away all reason, I saw you
in those sunlit fields, in those haystacks & rural ecstasies,
I saw you when the Cosmos was young & willing to be captured,
at least for the beauty of a brushstroke or an exquisite turn of phrase,
I saw you in those rough rustic landscapes, when I set my easel out amidst
the first dewdrops of each Rapture the mornings brought us, I remember
the billowing of your simple country dress, the wide sun drenched
straw brim of your summer hat, set at a reckless angle, with your
golden hair in waves down flowing across your shoulders,
I remember the sweet shy smile you always turned toward me,

even now across this great abyss of phantoms,
where nothing is as it was &
only Love Endures...

INTO RAPTURE

I watch
the river, & the exquisite
darkness of wild clouds rising,
I watch the river, & I know
the Cosmos calls me, right here & right now,
gently to your lips, I know each breath
is an exquisite miracle, a gift, an ecstasy
freely granted but at last at the price of every heartbeat
we so briefly thought was ours, I watch the river,
& I watch the soft settling of the sun across the mountains,
I exist in the exquisite scent of you, in the moment,
in the Magic, in the tingle of each fingertip that electrifies
this dangerous universe of flesh & blood & bone,
I thought I knew you, I thought I'd paid my dues & made my journey,
I thought I'd been a pilgrim, knight, & hungry lover,
I thought the Cosmos guided me, when at last I was ready,
to the sacred paradise where we lay & waited for the dawn together,
I thought I knew you, I thought the constellations were the erotic explosions
of each conflagration of our Beauty, I thought I would always meet you,
tide after tide, world after world, I thought my dues were paid,
my oaths fulfilled, my duties handed over, I thought the Wave might rise
& this world be swept away, but now I know the Earth endures,
& each Spirit shares its burden, at last like driftwood, lost & forgotten
on ancient shores, I know the spark is always lit, & time after time
we face the darkness, either embracing it like a Mystery,
or raging with the false security of candles, all will be as it must be
& the path leads ever onward into Rapture, Come embrace me, Love,
let my lips linger but a moment upon the rainbows of your eyelids,

let me dance slowly in this serene sensuality of your whispers,
let me lay my Dreams down, here & at last forever,
on the sanctity of your breast...

SHOW ME THE GODDESS

Just let me
embrace you, at least
a moment, just let me embrace you,
in the infinite Grace of your Heartbeat,
just let me embrace you, & let this tired world slip,
as exquisitely as my dreams, down through
the long lonely corridors of my fingertips, just let
the sands take me & scatter me heedlessly to the four great directions,
I am the world, & the first faint stirring of mystic Light
across the waters, I am the child, the warrior, the prince,
the ancient & amorous wizard, I am everything except
what you truly wished me to be, which was simple, profound & free,
I was everything except what this Cosmos needed,
forgive me my past indiscretions, my hollow promises,
my dances so drenched in Moonlight, I never saw the simple truth of it,
I never saw the river, so pure, so holy, so drenched with Stars,
I never saw the simple Rapture & supreme ecstasy of our eternal moments,
I just wanted to kiss you, & electrify my fingertips with the trembling
of your atoms, I was a knight who rode forth proud & conquered
each kingdom that just laughed & lured him even further
from the beaches where the Cosmos always waited sensual with Stars,
just embrace me & let me rest, just whisper sweet Mysteries
& I will believe you, I know who you are & where I'll always find you,
it's always here where my own sword wounds me, it's always here where
the twilight finds me, lost & yet never alone, it's here begging you
down through each conflagration of the galaxies, to somehow show me
the Goddess, at least beside this infinite blue ocean I'm always so scared
to swim in, just show me mercy & kiss me, just remember who
I might have been & cleanse me, with each glorious
miracle of your tears...

A REDEMPTION, IN OUR HEARTBEATS

I just
want to reach
someone, someone holy,
someone exquisite with
each dream I've forgotten I ever had,
I just want to reach out, with these arms
so rippled with the muscles of a thousand rebirths,
I just want to Dance but a moment
in the Light, in the Ecstasy, in the perfect
freedom of infinite Innocence, I just want to remember
each journey that somehow became a prison
of false expectations, I just want to meet you, to kiss you,
to caress you with these fingers aching to be Stars,
I just want to reach you, to taste you, to break free but yet
never say goodbye, I just want to know you, to stand beyond
each quest I ever sent myself upon, I just want to embrace you
& stay drunk forever with the elixir of each blossom yet shimmering
& naked before the dawn, I just want to meet you,
wherever you wait for me, I'm exhausted but still not broken,
nothing holds me, nothing chains me, it's just that everything's disappeared
& each Magic I once thought so important now seems like
ridiculous laughter in the wind, I hunger, I bleed & I thirst,
what more do you want from me, except this ecstatic aching of my Spirit
& now you have that too, I'm here & so are the trees, the meadows
& my memories, maybe the the past can be forgiven
& poverty is a sacred thing, in each Redemption of our heartbeats,
I'm just the pilgrim you always wanted, at least
I think you did, because that's what
I based my Life on...

LOVE RIDES UPON THE RAINBOWS

I'll just
come home,
to everything I never believed in,
I'll just come home & dance,
in this great conflagration of sunlight & wings,
I'll just come home & worry no more,
I'll just forsake everything & believe only
in the Light drifting down across the mountains,
I'll just live, I'll just dream as if truth trembled in every blossom,
I'll just embrace your whispers & follow you
through each dark & miraculous Midnight,
I'll just lay my burden down, my angers & my thousand
wounds of yesterday, I'll just let you hold me, I'll just let
my tears define me, I'll just go to war no more & finally
come tapping, at your cabin door, down in your amorous valley
& high on passion's windswept peak,
I'll just hear that wild storm rising, as if to sweep away the world,
I'll just count my moments & then forget them,
I'll just let my heartbeat bless me, as surely as if you kiss me on the brow,
I'll forsake all understanding & just grow slowly younger,
as if time & tide always smiled & renounced all former Magics,
I'll just embrace you as if Love finally rode upon the rainbows,
I'll just be everything I could never be, until this moment amid the galaxies,
when this world drifted from my shoulders & you finally
told me who I was, just before you touched me,
with the exquisite fingertips
of Stars...

LOVE IN A TIME OF HURRICANES

I knew
something was
coming, something new,
something dangerous,
I knew something was coming,
perhaps to sweep away the world,
I knew the storm was rising,
& the great exhilaration of the waves,
I knew the ravens called me
& each beautiful beast of the rainbows,
I knew all dreams were perfect, I knew my name
was somehow sacred & you were calling it,
I knew my roots were deep & yet not strong enough
to withstand the hurricane of your whispers,
I sought you in the stillness but now I know
the cities were swept glorious to the constellations,
each lost leaf calls me, each trembling of the grasses,
I know I kiss you in each conflagration of the sunsets,
I waited too late to ever escape you, even if I wanted to,
I know the stillness only deludes me, like a quiet & comforting
corner in a world of dangerous alleys, it doesn't matter if I whisper,
it doesn't matter if I howl, the Midnight is alive & I know it hunts me,
I know its hungers last forever & so do mine, I just raise this sword
& ride out into the endless arrows of the lightning,
all I see is wreckage & the vast coming of the sunbeams,
the ocean brought me & the olive branches of a thousand eagles
as Light scattered across the Waters, I had no plans,
no dreams, no purpose, but at least I
always sought you & I always
spoke the truth...

ONLY LOVE REDEEMS US

Only
Love redeems me,
only the holy coming of the night,
only Love redeems me, I who fought
a thousand battles in the endless horror
of misguided dreams, don't tell me anything,
don't preach, don't offer me any prophecies unless
you've truly seen the madness, the Magic is here
& the Light is open to us all, don't march toward my borders,
don't sail upon my oceans or scatter dark wings across my skies,
I've seen it all & finally the Stars embraced me,
I finally saw the evil, the pettiness & the outright lies,
the armies come & the armies go & still the thunder rolls the dice,
just have courage, friends, Lovers & even my enemies,
just stand & take a breath, just remember who you know we truly are,
just weep with me & release our poisons to the purification
of the air, the sea & the sky, just honour the heroines, the heroes
& the joyous jokers come to be our blessings, just have the honesty
to stand here naked, waiting for the holy eyes of the Dawn
to bless you with forgiveness, just learn to love the darkness
so suddenly alive with Nebulae, we here like the dust
& the wind always claims us, we're here to Love, Love
& Love again, until the final breaking of the Earth,
when we scatter into atoms & the Cosmos
smiles like it always has..

A DANCE OF SECRET STARS

I still believe,
& I want to lose myself in you,
in your Grace, in the mysteries
of the blue green ocean I see beckoning
in your eyes, perhaps I just imagine it,
the infinite depth of you, live after life after life
drifting back through the slow silver dance
of the secret Stars, perhaps I just imagine it, like poets
often do, perhaps you're the Goddess who always
eludes me except in the conjuring of my dreams,
perhaps you mock me, perhaps you unlock the pilgrim
always yearning in my Heart, for that wild & lonely whisper
of the Cosmos that finally reveals all things,
perhaps the river brought you, as the fleeting & most
precious gift of the season, perhaps the ravens are just laughing
& the rainbow bridge is always lost forever,
I'd forget you except I can't, I'd release you except you
keep moving closer, wary as a dancer but erotic in your fingertips,
I wish I could see you with your hair gently unbound & flowing
with the sunlight forever, we just sit here, uncertain but dangerous,
aching to embrace but lost in the way new Lovers often are,
hoping for tomorrow but hungry
for today...

ABIDE WITH ME

Just
abide with me,
here in the twilight
of everything that once had meaning,
just abide with me, in this slow
& holy healing of our battered Hearts,
just abide with me & watch the waters,
restless & unknowable in the sure
& certain darkness & coming of the Light,
just abide with me, fragrant with each promise
of the dawn still lingering in your hair, I want everything
you always were to me, immaculate, irreplaceable,
I want you to haunt me like you always did, with your Beauty
& breathless enthusiasm for everything exquisite
& ephemeral in Earth's fleeting teardrops, we broke our beliefs
& those promises so sacred to the pleasures of our youth,
we shattered everything with the careless bravery of childhood,
we're wounded now but still innocent in the ecstasies of our Spirits,
abide with me, but an eternity longer & perhaps I'll finally understand you,
it's quiet here & all Magics are possible, all secrets are revealed,
it might be the coming of Midnight or it might be the coming
of the Light, I just remember each kiss, each touch,
each erotic conflagration, I don't even want to try to understand it,
I just trust the Cosmos & the infinite rivers so vibrant & alive
with constellations, the galaxies are us & that's all we need to remember,
belief is a fragile thing & as elusive as a butterfly, I'll just bring you this cup
of galaxies & slowly shall we sip it, we'll just embrace here
in the silence so imminent with the music of our Heartbeats, we'll just

be here now & count our blessings, no matter how dangerous
they once seemed, we'll just count our blessings & abide a little longer,
as if it was our purpose, as if Life itself somehow
shimmered in our veins...

BENEATH THE HEARTBREAK OF THESE STARS

Here's
all I know,
& all I believe in,
here's all I am, empty at last
of all false vanity, desires & Dreams,
here's all I thought I was, all I hoped for,
& all I became at last, here's all I settled for,
here's all I strove for, all my battles,
all my useless expeditions, all my self inflicted defeats,
here's all I am, all I stood for in the end,
how I loved, how I hated, how I wheeled, how I dealt
my cards both honourably & surreptitiously from the bottom
of the deck, here's me as I am, as I was, & as I still might yet be,
here's me naked, here's me shimmering in dawn's glorious promises,
here's all my Magic, all my conjuring, all my escapades,
all my lost & lonely journeys, here I am, still unbroken but battered
by each storm I brought upon myself, I believed & I believed
& I believed again, & I rode each storm my Heart set against me,
here's me clinging on so fiercely to everything so ephemeral
& yet so exquisite in this world, here I am, golden boned & empty handed,
here I am, always waiting, always charging forward, here's me empty,
here's me full, never knowing which is the most sacred state,
here I am just loving you, just humbled by your Grace & yet always
hungry for the Mystery, here's me knocking yet again, at the invisible door
all poets pass through at the end, when nothing ever matters,
except the rainbows & the exquisite Rapture
of each last & shining breath...

A GIFT OF FRAGILE MERCY

I'll
come home
now, perhaps forever,
I'll come home now,
& wipe the dust at last from my boots,
I'll come home now,
& wash the salt & sea air from my hair,
I'll just lay this burden down,
this traveller's pack & map of endless wishes,
I'll just lay it all down & forget
I ever owned these simple things that in the end
became so heavy, I'll just rest here
& let tomorrow take care of itself, I'll forget the music,
the laughter, the sea of empty promises, I'll just
lie here & remember nothing, I'll forget my name, my Dreams,
my infinite fleeting desires, I'll just wait here in case
the Cosmos comes lightly looking with Dawn's lingering fingers
for any ancient knights amid these grasses, long lost & useless
except as a cautionary tale, told to children perhaps amid
the far flung constellations of the future, Be not like me & perhaps
you shall yet prosper, perhaps each orchard shall bloom
& you'll pause at least to savour it, perhaps you'll breathe the fragrance
of an Innocence eternal in its delight, we were human here
but perhaps you're beyond that now, perhaps your Spirits shine
& the comets dance upon the mountains, I always thought they did
& I had a thousand other Visions, perhaps you'll kiss the day
& the lips of your sweetest Lover, I did all that & it's still
yet possible, with the grace of an open Heart
& a fragile gift of Mercy...

BEAUTY, ON A BLACK BIKE

Just
release me,
kiss my eyelids & bless me
as if yesterday still had meaning,
as if Love still had freedom
& wisdom resided only in the heartbeat,
just release me but remember me,
don't blame me, I was what I was & that was just
an adventurer on this highway, just bless me
& throw no more stones, even if they seem so exquisite
they might almost be diamonds, just bless me
& let's forget the torrent of passing thoughts, let's just
finally listen & perhaps we'll finally find the cool centre
of this storm, the eye that so briefly opens & gazes
at last on the Cosmos, let's just listen & let it all go,
the truth, the passion, the lies, the stumbling & erotic fumbling
toward the Light, let's just agree to end this & yet embrace forever,
just kiss me & let me taste your flavours, the exquisite
complexity of your Rainbows, we danced a good dance, we lay
in a thousand summer meadows that honoured us with the erotic
fragrance of their fleeting ecstasy, this is my Song of Songs
& you are the Mystery who always haunted me, midnight after midnight,
when those fierce wolves howled & danger rattled at the windows,
I learned everything, sometimes on your lips & sometimes in your eyes,
I just worshipped you, in that faithful, faulty & all too human way,
I went upon a journey & there you were, always shining, always above me,
like the Star of all earthly imaginings, I have a host of stories that somehow
answer nothing except the questions no one knows, I saw you today,

gliding by, a sunlit Beauty on a steed as exquisite as the abyss
that dapples the dreams of the Nebulae, I saw you on your black bike,
as reckless as the Rapture of the darkness, already imminent
with Galaxies...

COME HOME, PILGRIM

I just
came calling,
home from the wars
& a pilgrim's endless journey,
I just came calling, my wounds almost hidden,
my eyes subtle & shaded with the endless oceans
the Stars sometimes sail upon,
I just came calling, somehow still smiling
in spite of everything, golden haired & silver threaded,
I just came calling, down by that river that swept it all away,
the anger, the anguish, the screech of eagles
& the ancient wisdom of ravens, I just came calling,
& midnight was in my voice & compassion was in my fingertips,
I hoped you believed me but at least we went dancing,
as if the Cosmos willed it, as if tomorrow was a lost & lonely dream
& Midnight held all the answers, I just came calling,
& for the exquisite infinity of that miraculous evening I truly believed it,
I became all things, all truths, all heroes, I became all things
merely to comprehend your Beauty, to worship you, to simply adore you,
to kiss your hand as gently as the first of your immortal Lovers,
I just came calling, with a host of phantoms & galaxies in my eyes,
I thought you truly saw me & for a moment I think that you did,
I heard the music & it always drew me to the highway,
I was the ghost of long remembering, the prince of all lost & lonely kingdoms,
I just came calling because I never stopped believing
& I knew lives dropped like pebbles into the storm of the constellations,
I just came home dressed in my ancient finery disguised as golden armour,
I came, I stumbled & I rose yet again, I knew no other Magic,
I just rested a moment on your Heartbeat & then the Dawn came calling,

I just came calling & dreamed a moment in your fragrance,
I just came calling, tipped my hat
& then I was gone...

PARADISE REMEMBERED

I never
knew you,
before the wars came calling,
I never knew you,
not truly, no matter how many times
we lay together, no matter how many sunsets
we spent in long & lingering kisses,
I brushed your cheek with fingertips now grown
so rough & ravaged, I searched for you,
when the searchlights lit the sky, when tomorrow
meant just another chance to disappear until danger
no longer sought me, I dreamed of you, in same way I yearned
for paradise, like a final breaking above the waters
& a holy breath of clear air & cleansing Light, I never knew you
except as a moment so fleeting it haunted me down through
each labyrinth of my lives, I just wait here in the rubble of all the galaxies,
in the mystery & mayhem of the Moonlight, you're so close
I can almost taste you & I remember each rainbow of your flavours,
the waters rise but still I seek the river so immortal
with the Stars, I thought I had a purpose & I asked nothing but your Grace,
I thought you still had Mercy, back then when each dawn was beautiful,
but now I know tomorrow never remembers & yesterday
seldom lingers long in each settling of the dust, all I hoped for in the end
was just the comfort of a heartbeat, laid so gentle against my own,
all I knew was that I loved you, then, today & forever,
before I even saw you...

A SUBTLE RISING OF THE RAINBOWS

I heard you
whisper, but I was
young & bold & foolish,
I heard you calling,
but I had a thousand lips to kiss
& a long & magical journey to undertake,
I heard you whisper so soft & subtle I thought
it was my heartbeat, it was long ago,
almost before this world began, I heard you whisper
but I thought it was the night wind, amorous
& enigmatic in its intentions, the road was long & the adventures
were many, I heard you coming but time after time
I thought it was the dawn, the shimmering of the dewdrops
or the trembling of a lover's breath, I heard you calling in each storm
that swept my sails uncharted to dangerous shores,
I thought I knew, at least who I was & what my purpose was,
I thought I knew but in the end all wisdom proved fickle & as forlorn
as the dust, I heard you whisper & I heard you yet again,
somewhere in the dark woods I always feared to enter, I heard you whisper
& then the sunlight came & I saw you dancing in the meadows,
I forgot my fears & they just dissolved into yesterday, long lost to time
& tide, I heard you & I waited, as if it was my own idea, as if I had a choice,
I heard you whisper & I felt the subtle rising of the rainbows,
as if your fingertips were electric with every promise of the constellations,
I never looked back, I saw the Cosmos & I knew it shimmered in your eyes,
I was a knight, a speck of a greater diamond, my flame burned bright
& now it ignites my pyre, I can leave it all behind now,
I can just rest here a moment, watching the river
& no longer wondering
where it's flowing...

NEVER LISTEN TO THE NIGHT WINDS

Listen,
in this last great
dance of the constellations,
in this last gentle hush before
the rising of the waters, just listen,
here on the first day & the last day,
here in the subtle ecstasy of the Dawn's light rising,
just listen & I'll whisper a moment in your ear,
just like I always have, here at the beginning & the ending,
just listen, because we have but a moment,
but a brief gathering of memories that cradle the atoms of our lives,
it's all ending & it's all beginning, it's a miracle
& just a heartbeat of the Cosmos, nothing lingers & yet
I believed so very ardently in you, I believed & I saw everything
my Spirit had always ached for, somehow shimmering in your eyes,
here at the edge of worlds all galaxies shatter & the sands
ascend to greater Suns, I came to you, too late & still not understanding,
I came to you beside this river of our lives already gathering rainbows,
you are so tall & strong & beautiful, but already the Earth shakes
beneath you, already the seasons fall away & Light trembles
at the edge of the oceans, dance while you can, My Love, & believe
in the thousand graces of the senses, just believe a moment longer & it might
almost seem a lifetime, never listen to the night winds when they howl
so lean & hungry, never listen because they might be lying,
never listen because all tales are told by a madman
& all true Lovers dream forever...

NAKED, IN THE GALAXIES

I had
this moment,
long ago & far away,
I had this moment, this revelation,
this moment of Glory,
I had this moment, at last
& when the Cosmos finally spoke,
I had this moment, this dream, this ecstasy,
I had this moment when all was as it should be,
when everything was revealed,
I had this moment, this Magic, this midnight
when the Stars swung close & whispered every secret,
I saw everything, I drifted, I flew, not as a creature
of flesh & blood & bone but as an angel,
I saw the great greening of the Earth & the miracle of the waves,
my fingers were electric & immense with constellations,
I guess you could say it was Paradise, undeserved perhaps
but exquisite in its unfolding, I saw you there,
as if peace had finally embraced me, as if we lay down finally
by the eternal river of the nebulae, I saw you naked in the galaxies,
I felt the infinity of my heartbeat & the sensual whirlpools of my atoms,
everything urged me onward, as if eternity smiled & beckoned,
finally just a breath beyond the comets, the sun rose & fell & rose again,
& the wild salt wind rippled through the waves of your fragrant hair,
we were the Lovers, dangerous, immaculate & unimagined,
I felt the sunlight, like the first & final Rainbows
breaking across the waters, I knew the worlds
would end today or somehow
be forgiven...

A WILD WAVE, SINGING

This is
how it was,
this is how the Song began
& how it ended,
this is the truth of it, this is the world
we lived in, danced in, loved in,
this is the strange high shimmering music of the Stars
a moment before all mirrors shattered,
this is the story, the fragrance of summer meadows
& the crystalline glitter of winter's miraculous palaces,
this is who we were, these are our dreams, our hopes, our fantasies,
this is the subtle electric touch of our fingertips
yearning for the constellations, we had so little time except
the eternity between our heartbeats, we had so little Magic
except each exquisite ecstasy of our breaths, perhaps we'll be forgotten,
perhaps we'll be remembered, but as long as the dawn rises
& Light sings as it rises radiant above the waters I believe we will linger,
I feel each spark of the Cosmos miraculous within you,
each flicker of the flame so ethereal & yet so present in this
glorious gathering of flesh, & blood & bone, I believe in each revelation,
each beauteous redeeming of our atoms, we are what we are
& as the nebulae made us, tomorrow always promises but in truth
only the slow sensual serenity of the Midnight delivers, we're just here now,
& embracing in this moment as precious as the trembling of the last & final
dewdrop, this is my Song of Songs, my death, my life, my Redemption
& rebirth, this is the wild wave singing, & the green wisdom of the forests,
we live, we live, & we live again, that's all I know,
when I watch the river & wonder
if I'm dreaming...

IN YOUR NAME, GODDESS

Once
I knew you,
once I knew you & I lived
for your whisper,
I yearned for you, breathed for you,
grew Magic & wild eyed
just to win you, once I knew you & your eyes
consumed me, the barest glimpse of you
was like an ecstasy, like a bright Star breaking
across a pilgrim's long & lonely night,
once I believed in you, yearned for you, wove a thousand
Dreams around you, once every dance I danced
was an ecstasy in your honour, I believed in you, in your promise
& the strength of your Heartbeat, we went upon a journey,
or at least we started on one, we were bold, mysterious
& wreathed in the erotic mystery of ancient Magic, we had the forest,
the meadows & the wild wind fragrant with the scent
of the most sensual of blossoms, we had our secret, our desire,
our Mystery, & I thought it would go on forever,
I thought I would always meet you, high on that rainbow bridge,
wild amid the galaxies, I thought I would always meet you
& the journey would go on forever, I thought I would always meet you
but now I sometimes wonder, who are you & why are you talking this way,
we had a sacred purpose, a gift we intended to grace the world with,
it was sacred, it was sensual, with the erotic intensity of the Cosmos,
we were never to be small, or common or ordinary, you said it was a joyous
secret, a conjuring, a treasure we set amid the constellations to guide
all once & future Lovers, you grow more beautiful but your words seem
strange & as fleeting as the moment, where is everything we dreamed of,
I still believe & I know there's no one like you, just remember who we were

& where we were going, just come to me as naked & profound as a Goddess,
don't bargain with me, I've moved beyond that, I stand here waiting
& always in awe of you, don't make me a common man,
just listen & you'll hear each exquisite syllable
written in your name...

A WILD WOLF HOWLING

Everything's
just a joke, at least today,
everything's just a joke & it's
got me laughing, I thought I knew a secret
somehow sublime in its revelation,
I thought I knew a secret but that was just
the Cosmos smiling, just the constellations grinning
& saying, Hey wait a minute, think it over,
I thought I was on a journey but actually the truth is always now,
shimmering beneath the bloodied bandages of all our battles,
you're no one special & yet you are, unique & yet just
another fleck of a million joyous Rainbows, climb high & the starlight
claims you, lay low & the Earth smiles & steals your Heartbeat,
nothing is as it was & yet everything is as it will be,
you think you're beautiful & then suddenly everything else is,
the unseen world becomes the seen & all dances finally end
although the music goes on forever, I keep thinking that you love me
but that's just this ridiculous yearning, this wild wolf howling
at the inconstant Moonlight, tomorrow I'll just smile & feel the breezes,
the shimmering of Light across the waters, I play this game over & over,
not because I want to but because I have to, tomorrow is always a miracle,
in its small & yet so infinite moment, I'd shake you loose
but somehow I need the danger, the electricity of Lovers, star crossed,
long lost, & yet so unaware of everything except the electric bridge
of fingertips, joining battered Spirit to battered Spirit,
& always ecstatic to earn another day...

GREEN EYES, BIG OCEAN

I just
walked in,
I just walked in & nothing
was the same, ever,
I just walked in & there I was,
lost in the ocean of you, in the sea salt taste
of infinity & unknown horizons,
I just walked in & fear was almost forgotten,
dreams were almost real, I said goodbye & I said hello,
who I became was never clear except when I kissed you,
except when heroic imaginings overwhelmed me,
I believed in everything & Magic was alive,
at least in the electric embrace you caught me in, in the exquisite
blue green infinity of your eyes, who you really were
never mattered, all I ever saw in you was Beauty & the indescribable
inner grace of a Goddess, perhaps the Cosmos kissed me
& it was in the taste of you, in the erotic shiver of your skin as ecstasy
mounted, you were all I knew or ever wanted to,
the nights were long & the days were ever brighter, lost in sunlight
& the beckoning of the river that drew us onward, gently, irresistibly toward
the shimmering dances of the constellations, I never loved you
except I always did, even before I met you, whatever I am now I am
because I met you, because we always went dancing, because I lost you
& found you & lost you again, sometimes in the shadows,
sometimes in the Moonlight, we were who we had to be, you were young
& strong & proud, & I was ancient & knew the journey, I could have
saved myself but I didn't want to, I had some wisdom once
but I just tossed it to the ravens, let tomorrow come as it must,
nothing means anything anymore, except when I reach out
& touch you, here in the miracle
of the moment...

INTO YOUR GREEN EYES

I'm just
here now, & so are
you, & this is the great dance
as the Cosmos wills it,
I'm just here now, lost in the moment,
in the sunlight breaking across the waters,
I'm here, I'm powerful & free of all previous disasters,
I'm just here beneath the blue sky, dancing
& dangerous in this, the most perfect of all dangerous
& perfect summers, I'm just here, powerful, proud
& careful as a lamb, I'm just here because you're here, I know
that now, I feel it in every electron inherent in my being,
why we were chosen I know not & I care even less, you come to me
& I watch you, mesmerized in the miracle of the absolute Beauty
of our beings, in the infinite Grace of even your fingertips
fluttering so lightly across my Dreams, nothing you say has any meaning,
nothing you do has any purpose except that the nebulae glow
within your Heartbeat & all Bliss waits trembling in the ecstasy
of your breath, blind fools love you but only I am ready for you, only I
am ready & able to reach you, here on this last & moonlit journey that leads
so inevitably to the Stars, I'm always waiting here, in each secret of a Kiss
& embraces as yet unknown, there's knights & knights & knights
& fair & beautiful maidens but it's all just a shimmering of Rainbows,
a Rapture fleeting & profound, I see you, I sense you, I catch
the scent of immortal orchards, we'll just lie a moment here, body to body
& each Spirit subtle & so shimmering within Spirit, the time is now
& I step forward as the one hero fit to Love you, I'm here
& you're here & that's all that really matters, we're innocent & naked
& the wild wolves prowl, but at last I no longer fear them, I no longer even

need my weapons, the oceans are wide & the galaxies are vast,
just reach out & draw me under, into your green eyes, into this darkness,
into these whispers & the rising
of the Light...

IN A THOUSAND LOVER'S WAYS

Sometimes
I loved you,
sometimes I hated you,
sometimes I didn't even know who you were,
sometimes I lived only for your caress,
for your whisper, for the infinite miracle of your green eyes,
sometimes I just forgot you & went drifting through dark
& dangerous alleys, sometimes Magic was all I needed,
whether your own or someone else's, sometimes I came knocking,
bruised, broken & penitent in a thousand Lover's ways,
sometimes I just cast you aside, sometimes you deserved me,
sometimes you didn't, it was all as the river flowed & as the Cosmos
willed it, I see that now & I accept it, I embrace it,
the miracle was the moment & we were the dancers caught so irrevocably
in the music, just release me or embrace me, heal me, help me,
take to those wild & mystic places, those strange & secret landscapes
of your Spirit, I bleed & I know you are wounded almost unto death,
we were the Rapture & the nebulae embraced us, at least for a moment,
at least for a shimmering spinning of this Earth as it bloomed
amid the constellations, I still believe & somehow that makes me a Hero,
perhaps tomorrow will linger at least for yet another exquisite
breath of summer meadows & all that we truly might have been,
I was a fool & I realize that now, but you believed in me & that almost
makes you a greater one, we just came here open hearted,
we just came here innocent & alone, & for that we touched the rainbows,
we just kissed & that was the beginning
& the end...

ALL EXQUISITE & BROKEN THINGS

There's
nothing here
holding me, no chains,
no miracles left to believe in,
there's no Mystery, no Magic, no madmen
left dancing, there's nothing here
holding me, nothing left to dream of, to scheme for,
there's nothing left bold, bright & beautiful,
there's nothing left except that everything is,
fears always hold sway but a moment, shadows always rule,
at least a heartbeat before the great rising of the Light,
fear always rules, & fury, & the fierce tides
still rising to sweep away the Stars, I hear the music
& the music always hears me, here, right now, in the immortality
of the moment, these chains shall not bind me,
these hesitations, these pathetic hatreds, desires & misplaced loyalties,
the Cosmos will always call me, I know that now,
the Cosmos will always heal me because all small, broken
& lonely things are always embraced with the most tender & exquisite Mercy,
perhaps I loved you & I loved unwisely, perhaps tomorrow
is just the shifting sand of yesterday's smiling mistakes,
I'm here for a purpose & I struggle daily to fulfill it, in your kiss,
in your caress, in the exquisite shimmering constellations of your body,
I was made to be passionate, I wasn't made to be perfect,
I just arrived to Love you, & that's all there is,
or ever will be...

DANCE WITH ME, GREEN EYES

Come
dance with me,
I don't care
about the bad days,
I only care about the real days,
the moments with Heart,
the dawns to dusk with Music in them,
with Magic, with Grace,
come dance with me, right here,
before right & wrong steals us away again,
each to our separate silences, come dance with me here,
in this place the Cosmos loves, on these grasses
sweet with summer, just embrace me
in your green eyed storm of golden hair, just feel
the naked rhythm of our Spirits, the Joy, the Bliss so
sacred to the Earth, tomorrow never comes
except in the next exhilaration of our breath, I don't
know you, I never did & I never will except in the Mystery
of your touch, as electric as ecstasy & as subtle as the Buddha's rose,
just dance with me & we'll just let it last forever,
we'll just let ourselves loose & see if the galaxies kiss us,
the river calls & the horizons are widespread & infinite,
just dance with me, I'm lost in the yearning of your eyes,
all dreams are dangerous & this is mine, just to see you, just to touch you,
just to meet you amid the rainbows & taste the colours
upon your lips, all I want is everything & then a little bit more,
I want to feel the fires within you, I want to reach the flesh & bone
& soul that sustains you, I want to know you, to touch you, to win you,
just dance with me, here, just dance with me & we'll see
where our madness takes us...

LET YOUR HEARTBEAT OPEN

Just
wait here,
at least a moment,
just abide with me, just wait here,
at the beginning & ending
of all worlds, just wait here, with me,
wordlessly embracing & our eyes
upon the constellations, just wait here,
just listen, to the night wind & the miracle of the moment,
just abide with me, here where the Cosmos calls us,
here where the starlight sees us, just open your Heartbeat,
here with me forever, eternal & yet finally young & never changing,
wait here, with me, within me, deeper than our words
& declarations that seemed so precious, once, before we
learned to listen to the silence that defines all sound, this is it, this is us,
who we were & every miracle we're bound for, let us
bow here & pray with each great glittering conflagration of our atoms,
let us be here, truly, completely & at last, let us listen, linger
& perhaps even learn a little something, a wisp of the joy
the nebulae nightly know, we're breathless here & yet our lungs
glow with exquisite air, this is it, this is the ecstasy all Magic finally leads to,
here it comes, the twilight, the Midnight, & the shimmering of Dawn
across the waters, we're new here, we're naked & reborn,
the dust is like the weary breaking of all forgotten promises, just listen,
just take my hand & don't even think about it, don't imagine
& don't remember, this is what it is & always will be, just wait here
& feel it coming, something deeper, something depthless,
it's closer & it's smiling, it's like a rainbow, like a healing,
like a great hush that somehow
holds our world...

HERE I ALWAYS AM

I'll just
say goodbye,
at least until a tomorrow
that never comes, I'll just
say goodbye, at least until dawn
breaks across the mountains, what I was
I no longer am, who I was I never knew,
I just came, I lost, I won, I breathed exquisite air,
the old mysteries whisper & dreams seem
aching to unfold, I'll just say goodbye & bid this foolishness
farewell, I'm no Hero & I never was, I sought
the lone Star gleaming, I took the path untraveled,
but now every destination seems the same, I conjured for you,
I brought my Magics & spun fabulous tales, I thought
I could win you & then I wondered why I wanted to,
it's all over & yet I know it's just beginning, the Earth shifts
& I feel the trembling of the oceans, all is not how it was
& nowhere near as it yet may be, I feel you always, in my Heart,
my mind & my Spirit, I know you're not even near me & yet
you never leave me, I see you in those summer fields, a thousand years ago,
golden haired, green eyed, the vision that always sustained me,
the scent, the beauty, the orchards, the comets bursting in the night,
to have found you in this place almost breaks me, here in this modern world,
here in this smoke & flame & ash that seemingly never ceases,
I don't belong here & yet the Cosmos calls me, the river brought me
& now I dance beneath the Moonlight, sometimes I ramble,
sometimes my words fly & I remember how to Love,
it all just flows, over & over again,
& here I always am...

CROSSROADS

Here
at the crossroads
all things begin & all things end,
here at the crossroads
the Stars lean close & the Cosmos whispers,
here at the crossroads we're born, we Love, we die,
we dance, over & over again, wrapped in the rainbows
& the infinite canyons that cradle the nebulae,
we're here, we dance, we die, & then we're reborn,
the Moonlight always rises & scatters infinite diamonds
across each raging of the waves, we're here, we're brave, we're bold,
nothing means anything & yet everything does,
here in this ecstasy, this Rapture of this & all possible worlds,
we're here, we blossom, we wither, we rise again, season after season,
we're innocent & yet dangerous as children, squabbling amid
the shimmering bliss of the Earth, we're just in love, we're just in lust,
we're just here waiting by the shore, watching the constellations
& beating on our drums, we paint our bodies, we glorify our dreams
but in the end the river claims us all, just sit with me, here,
at least a moment, just gaze into these war weary eyes, we're the past,
the future, & all the Magic shimmering on the oceans in between,
I hear you, I touch you, each atom I exist in adores you,
I'm old but now I come again, I hear the wind but I'm never sure
what it's saying, somehow I know it's always enough,
no matter the road we all ultimately go down, somehow
I just keep believing, like a madman, like an angel,
I just keep believing that it all has some nameless meaning,
or even if it doesn't I still don't care, I hear the music
of the galaxies & that's always
almost wisdom...

GOODBYE, GREEN EYES

I never
thought I'd write this,
so I guess I'm just human after all,
I guess I'm just the fool I always feared I was,
I believed in you, or at least I thought I did,
I believed in you, as if you were a gift the Cosmos
secretly bequeathed me, I thought I had a purpose, a glory,
a meaning that somehow set me apart from all others,
I thought the galaxies loved me & I think maybe they did,
in their infinite Mercy, I think they kissed me on the brow
in the way they kiss all pilgrims, all poor fools destined to wander forever
in a Mystery there's no possibility they'll ever truly fathom,
I believed in you, I saw you as I thought you were & that proved to be
my great undoing, we are all as we are, no better & no worse,
children of the river & atoms scattered from the Stars, you bewildered me,
you mesmerized me, but only because I still thought dreams were real,
that Beauty was still possible when the Spring winds blew,
I took you as the Magic I was never supposed to steal, I just believed
& felt the power, the conjuring, the dawn each Hero feels when he
sets sail upon the tide, I felt the Goddess knew me & came to me, gradually,
in your thousand incomprehensible ways, I accepted each wound,
each miracle, each endless repetition of the mundane, I embraced it all
as a holy path & I tried to light the world, I tried to light the world
but I forgot that was too great for the smallness of my Spirit,
I just believed you were set apart, a guide, a signpost,
a great revealing, but now I know it was all my madness,
& you're just happy as you are, a simple maiden
& the gift of a fleeting summer, I wish I'd known that,

& I apologize, but only for being a madman,
never for being
a Poet...

NO SPIRIT HAS A BOUNDARY

I had
some dreams, once,
I had some dreams,
some aches, some pains, some yearnings,
I had some dreams & I thought
only you could heal me for a moment,
I thought you had the touch, the Grace,
the deep butterfly wings of incomprehensible Beauty,
I believed in you & that's really all it was,
a trust, a confidence, a faith so simple it might
almost have been a child's, I had no fear, I felt the strength
that only Heroes feel, sometimes at least when they sight
what might at last be the promised shore, I knew you were waiting,
somewhere behind the complex & varied textures of my Life,
I knew the constellations dangled you, strange, sensual & yet always
awash with sunbeams, just slightly beyond the electric hunger
of my fingertips, I knew the Cosmos whispered, almost imperceptibly
but with a sly insistence, in each golden wave of your hair
as it spilled down across your shoulder, I knew you were Magic,
a gift of the river & as easily borne away, I forgot everything, except
my madness I guess, I forgot everything that my journey had
reluctantly taught me, the hard won victories of a thousand useless battles,
I just believed again that Love was infinite & lingered down
through the disasters of the ages, I just believed the Spirit had no boundaries,
& that the ecstasy of flesh, & the great raptures of the Heartbeat were
always somehow still possible, I believed you were a Goddess
& that was my great downfall, I became drunk on you & descended
into fever dreams, I was young & strong & beautiful,
a least while I felt the power, which was
only when you kissed me...

121

A WILD WING LOST

I thought
I could come to you,
I thought I was strong enough,
wise enough, I thought I breathed
the same exquisite air you did,
I thought my wounds had made me holy,
I thought my words were like a Magic
you would ache to hear, I thought my fears
were silent & dreams could never outrun me,
I thought you would tell me your Spirit's deepest secrets
when we lay alone in our sensual Midnights,
I just rode in & carried you off to that far & fragrant shore
where new constellations nightly gather, I fought for you,
against all others & against myself, I knew you were
stolen treasure, a wild wing already lost to new horizons,
I held you close in each silence between our heartbeats when I knew
all miracles were yet possible, I knew the day would come,
I knew the rivers would rise & sweep us both away,
but each moment was an ecstasy that seemed to shimmer forever,
like the ever changing mysteries of Light upon the waters,
the great reckoning came & went & came again, but still we embraced,
still we set sail bravely into the unruly raptures of your Eyes,
you were the blue green ocean I never truly understood except as
a Beauty I always remembered, like a pilgrim does, when memories
keep crowding closer & salvation seems close at hand,
even if it's just the flicker of far off galaxies, elusive
with a fading hint of tomorrow...

SAD EYES, BENEATH THE MOON

I don't care
who's right, who's wrong,
who's the fool, who behaved badly,
I don't care because here
in this great twilight of the world each breath
is precious, each heartbeat is renewed,
by the grace of a loving Cosmos, forget who we think we are,
our pride, our shame, our slings, our arrows,
they're children's toys, just come to me & I will come to you,
open handed, bare breasted, naked & completely vulnerable here,
beneath the rainbows, I only loved you & that was just
the beginning & the end of it, everything else was smoke & mirrors,
the fear of somehow failing you, the lust so subtle I almost
couldn't comprehend it, you were tall, beautiful & proud, a Goddess
for a thousand years, but still a child barely grown into the Beauty
so suddenly thrust upon you, of course you made mistakes, who could
blame you, who could comprehend the ecstasy you struggled so hard
to understand, there was only silence, when you went looking for wisdom,
only cheap & tawdry answers to your heartbeat's deepest questions,
I tried to save you & instead I only lost myself, what can I say,
I just love you, love you, love you, but even that just means nothing,
we're locked in a struggle I never understood or wanted,
we're just lost on these rough seas, strangers
still longing to embrace & yet
lost beneath the Moon...

123

A KISS CAN ALWAYS SAVE US

Silence
always claims me,
at last & then forever,
silence always calls me, claims me,
becomes me, I know the words,
the incantations, the songs, I know the whispers
all trembling Hearts ache to hear,
I know them, like the Stars I keep hidden in my pockets,
I know the words & yet the Cosmos always
steals them, the Moonlight always whispers them,
as if they belong to the last & most enduring of our graceful
silver dances, I'm not who I am or even who I appear to me,
I'm just the river & the exquisite hush of twilight all true
Lovers yearn for, I'm always here, in each winter, spring
& exquisite summer of your breath, I'm always beside you, here,
when the cool winds blow & autumn seems so imminent,
I'm everything you dreamed of & yet I dance here like this clown,
this jester, this prophet whose visions just linger a moment on the walls,
like the graffiti of humble Galaxies lost in lonely alleys,
I see you & I know you, at least sometimes, when the soft breezes
caress me & I rest a moment by the river that cradles us all,
we go forward to broken kingdoms & the ruins of all who rose before us,
perhaps we're smiling monkeys, perhaps we're angels
amid the rainbows, in the end it never matters, we're just here
a fleeting moment, to no purpose but our own, the nebulae forget us
& fly upon their glorious journeys, I came here to save you,
at least that's what I hope sometimes, when I realize it's a human mystery,
magic in this brief & glorious Rapture, when a kiss
can always save us...

ONLY A KISS CAN SAVE YOU

I made
some mistakes,
more than a few of them,
I made some mistakes, some disasters,
some blunders, I took some wrong roads,
I went on some dubious journeys,
I was a pilgrim always deluded, always turning
toward the false miracles of pride & vanity,
I was always to blame & yet maybe not always so,
I just kept believing & that has to count for something,
I kept my faith, I fought my fears & always danced beneath the Stars,
once I wanted everything, but now I just want those
big dreams again, those visions, those miracles, those Magics,
youth is long gone & yet I linger here, simple & loving as a child,
I always believe & go forward, innocent into the Light,
call me a fool, a rogue, a rascal just trying to cover his tracks,
but throw your own stones first because all my wars have gradually ended,
I blame no one, even the monsters I never asked for,
either you hear the constellations or you dwell here forever in silence,
the Cosmos whispers simple secrets & at last I can finally hear them,
I watch the river & I drift in wayward dreams that always at last lead me
somewhere, I'm just who I am & that's all I ever will be, the galaxies
keep shining within my atoms, I didn't intend this, I just wanted to smile
& somehow grow ancient & wise at last, I guess that never happened
but there's always next time, right now I just want to love you,
the Midnight is always our friend, like the deep
sensual abyss between the Stars, where everything
is forgotten & only a kiss
can save you...

EACH DEWDROP CALLS US

Between
now & forever,
I always believe Love is waiting,
I always believe the Cosmos
smiles & kisses us lightly on the brow,
between now & forever,
I still somehow see you dancing, young,
lithe & beautiful, as if the seasons loved you,
as if time had no dominion, I believe in nothing now
except the great Mercy I finally feel embracing me,
I believe in nothing now, except those promises
I freely offered, except those arms I willingly embraced,
this pilgrim's life is over except that it somehow never is,
dawn always rises & the thousand fragrances of summer still call me
out beneath the Stars, sometimes to meet you, sometimes to mourn you,
sometimes to realize it's really all just one & the same,
the galaxies are still so silent when each dewdrop quivers with anticipation,
I still remember when we lay here, so innocent & naked
of all but the purest of all desires, I still remember when we lay here,
I so lost in the long cascading waves of your hair,
falling so softly like the fingers of amorous twilight across my chest,
that was long ago & yet it was only yesterday, a miracle so profound it
somehow shook the Earth & shimmered forever like Light breaking
across the waters, it was the Rapture that spins the nebulae
& weaves rainbows so intricate above the meadows,
between now & forever I'm still here waiting, as if your whisper
could always find me, no matter the Magic that finally turned against us,
no matter what you gave me I always wanted more, I'm brave that way,

I always believe ecstasy endures, even if the river rises
& dreams seem broken & briefly
swept away…

WILD BENEATH THE STARS

I'm lost here,
but who cares about that,
it's all part of it, it's all the great dance
& the music just keeps on playing,
we're here, we love, we die, over & over while
the constellations still revolve above us,
there's no reason except the pure & perfect Magic of it,
the Harmony, the Grace, the Beauty,
either accept it or go down bleeding into oblivion & the dust,
I'm just lost here but I never feel that way, I always stand up smiling,
I always remember each kind Heart who loved me,
each amorous adventurer who shared an eternity in our kisses,
I was always hungry but I never knew what for,
I was always fierce upon the highway & wild beneath the Stars,
I was everything except what I wanted to be,
I just heard the wind & the strange whispers of the galaxies,
I heard the wild wolves following & the occasional wings of angels,
I'm just lost here & yet I always know where I'm going,
& that's to the final mystery of each shimmering horizon,
sometimes you love me, sometimes you betray me,
sometimes you believe me because I lay my head on your breast
& whisper of each miracle I believed in, when the seasons
whirled around me & all I knew was chaos, we're nothing but immortal
children, either believe or call me a liar, both are equally true,
I'm just the knight you called, sometimes when Midnight was a madness
& something was scratching at your window,
though you never knew
what it was...

ALL WILD THINGS FINALLY EMBRACE

I'll
always be here,
in my body, bones or my Spirit,
I'll always be here,
come rain, wind, or darker weather,
I'll always be here, like a whisper, like a ghost,
like a phantom faintly glimpsed
when you come trembling to the wild wood
& the Moonlight, all my weapons are buried now,
like the lost treasure of all golden things,
tell me where the kings are now, & the princes of this Earth,
ask me where are the mighty & I'll tell you,
they sleep, long lost & forgotten, with every dream fools ever had,
I was just a Poet, just a simple man who loved you,
I rode too fast & I swooped too low, I flew too high & the sunlight
confused me with the mystery of the rainbows,
I was a dreamer & I always dreamed I'd find you, I always
hoped I'd meet you, down by the banks of the cool sweet river where
all wild things finally embrace, I always thought I'd meet you
where all atoms mingle & nothing is forbidden, I truly believed
nothing was impossible, even that you might somehow love me at the last,
well at least I'm free of my delusions now & I see the Goddess everywhere,
my Heart is at last free to dance unbidden, free to kiss at will
& with true erotic fervour, you were just a flicker of the Starlight
& I but the archer with a sacred arrow, perhaps I might have pierced you
but in the end that might have slain you, who knows the Magic
& the mischief we sometimes make, when we're young & first set
foot on that fatal highway, that leads at last to
the crumbling edge of the Earth, & the arms
of a smiling Cosmos…

129

GUIDE ME HOME

Now
that you're here,
so dark eyed & beautiful,
now that you're here, now that
you're watching, intrigued, expectant,
now that the Cosmos smiles
& so subtly spreads its wings, now that dreams are here,
now you're waiting, reaching out, yearning,
shimmering, exquisite in the expectation of starlight,
now that the Magic hears us & comes so
slyly shining through the electricity of our atoms,
now that you're here & I'm here & the mystic door is opened,
between two Spirits, between two Souls so disparate
& yet so quickly entwining, now that the Midnight already
seeks us & braids your hair with sensual perfume,
now that we both know this Love is dangerous & foolish & careening
wildly into disaster amid this, the greatest of all possible Raptures,
now that we know you're young & beautiful
& lithe with the grace of all earthly innocence, now that we know
that our touch is amorous & fully intended, now that we know you break
a thousand hearts but only I hold the handful of galaxies
you've always yearned for, now that a kiss is already erotic in its intensity,
now that wisdom warns us but we go dancing anyway,
now that the end & the beginning & the flame might rip apart this world,
now that your ebony eyes embrace me, now that the dark waves
of your hair haunt me, I just give thanks & accept it, I seek
only Beauty & I always accept it, danger means nothing,
you're the Lover always waiting, alone at the farther shore,
lighting the beacon to guide me
Home...

A BUTTERFLY WHO HAUNTS ME

I'm
just here,
waiting & I don't
even know what for,
maybe for another great turning
of the constellations, maybe for the rise
of yet another new & shining Earth,
I'm just here, waiting, wondering & wandering,
I know all the highways by now, all the signposts,
all the lost & lonesome valleys, all the comets
above the mountains, I'm just here, the same as I always was,
part of me a hero & part of me a child, whatever truth I knew
I squandered with the rolling dice of fleeting earthly wisdom,
once I was tall & beautiful & proud, or at least that's what they told me,
but like everyone else I felt it all slip through my fingers
like the shimmering dust of Stars, maybe I'm a phantom,
maybe I'm immortal, I never knew & it doesn't matter anyway,
in the end all I can do is love you, sometimes in the Moonlight,
sometimes in the quivering of the wild wood when old ghosts walk,
I know all the flavours of your kisses but still they taste so sweet
& sensual & profound, I no longer even try to guess which Magic made me,
whether the infinite outstretched arms of the Cosmos
or the intricate beauty of the atoms, the key is here somewhere,
maybe in the miracle of your dark eyes, maybe in the sunlit kaleidoscope
of your wings, you're the butterfly who always haunts me,
just let me see you naked, just let me see you free & shining
in this, either the first day or the last day,
of all once & future
dreams...

AN ECSTASY ON YOUR LIPS

I sometimes
wonder, if you're
listening or if you
even care, I sometimes wonder
but then I look at the intricacies
& strange storms my own Heart goes through,
we're all just dancing here, ever ready
to be shattered in the deep crystal silences
where our Spirits wander between our heartbeats,
I always loved you, not in the common way,
but in the exalted way, in the miracle of our atoms,
in the Mystery of our midnights when
we somehow owned the sky & the constellations
smiled & spoke to us, I never knew you & I don't know you yet,
all I know is that you were the maiden who suddenly
came dancing, sensuous & raven haired, out of the mystery
of the endless oceans, without you I would have been a simple man,
fulfilled & yet unsatisfied in my purpose, without you
all the ancient Magics would have been vague & half remembered,
but that was long ago & now here I am, reborn & invincible,
at least for as long as the Cosmos wills it, I gaze at
those big beautiful dark eyes & I wonder what galaxies shimmer
so secretly in their depths, I'm whispering in your ear now,
as if our touch was almost imminent, just come to me open,
radiant in your Spirit, naked in the wildflowers, I'm done with beads
& baubles & the lure of shiny things, we met once, in the sacred groves
of the Stars, in the light laughter of summer's sweet nymphs bathing,
we met once & here we are again, I just want to embrace you
& taste the truth like an ecstasy
on your lips...

LOVERS IN THE LONG NIGHT

Everything
was broken, once,
everything was broken
& then came back stronger,
tomorrow is never forever & neither
is yesterday, it's always just the moment & infinite
in its rainbows, everything was broken
so that our children could rise & the Earth could blossom,
nothing is as it seems & even the Stars sometimes wonder,
here I am as I always was, a hero, a knight
& a fool always rapping at your window, you've loved me
a thousand times & yet I still don't know you, except perhaps
in my dreams but I knew long ago that Moonlight can't be trusted,
I searched for you, beside each great river of the world,
in the storm, in the rain, in the wild & cleansing wave of each tempest
come to wreck the orchards, I was here, I searched, I listened,
I was here & that's all each of us can say, no matter
how long the kisses linger, perhaps paradise is always elusive,
perhaps redemption is at hand, the danger is always dancing,
the Midnights are always pure, in the end the truth is always
just what you long for, I always see it in Beauty
& that's all I truly believe in, because that's
how the Cosmos whispers, into my ear
when you embrace me, & I know
the night is long…

AN INFINITY IN YOUR ARMS

Maybe
you've seen me,
either in your dreams
or passing by you on the highway,
maybe you've seen me
beside the mysteries of the oceans
or laughing wild out in the deserts,
perhaps you've even kissed me & felt the Stars
I keep hidden in my fingertips, perhaps you've known me,
believed in me, even thought we would build a Life together,
or perhaps you've danced with me in the wild wood
& made Love with the Moonlight watching, perhaps you've lived with me,
died with me, perhaps even healed me, perhaps you've seen me go down,
fighting, battle after battle & war after war, perhaps you've seen me
triumphant, broken or just passing through this earthly journey,
unnoticed & alone, perhaps you know me, finally & at last,
as who I truly am, perhaps you'll hear the river & finally meet me there,
beneath the wide open arms of the constellations, perhaps we'll finally meet,
again & again & again, Lovers until the end of time,
we are the dust & the shining glory of atoms, the Cosmos needs us
& no storm will break us, we're the exquisite miracle
born of tiny trembling creatures, grown to giants in our imaginations,
if I can make you smile then my moments are truly worth living,
I just want to rest a moment, against the ecstasy
of your Heartbeat, I just want to keep you
in my arms...

GOODBYE, GREEN EYES

Maybe
you came to test me,
maybe you came to heal me,
maybe the Moonlight
just smiled & thought it would
take me dancing, I wanted you with
that exquisite foreboding of disaster
I was always so sure would never touch me,
you should be mine, at least for the ecstasy of a heartbeat,
at least for a great & perfect turning of the Earth,
you should be mine but now I know you never will be, you belong
with each dream the Cosmos weaves to tempt poor pilgrims
into Rapture, I could break you down & I guess I did that,
in the slow & subtle conflagration of our sweetest summer meadows,
I could consume you in those flames but I take no comfort in the ashes,
we just lay a moment, naked in the realms where constellations
love freely on the Earth, perhaps you hear me screaming,
so silently in my memories of what might have been, perhaps your tears
will finally raise a river that will drown me, I'm wounded
but you'll never see me bleeding, I'll just take this treasure stolen
from our kisses & sail on to fragrant shores, unknown & yet so familiar
once again, grief will never break me but Beauty always does,
you overplayed your hand but I just rolled the dice, what a couple of fools,
we heard the river calling but were too stupid to answer,
now we take comfort in the arms of various strangers, but that'll never
be the answer, perhaps I could have been gentler, perhaps
you could have been less proud, sometimes I feel
like laughing but it has a hollow,
bitter sound…

DANGER, DISASTER OR HIGH WATER

Maybe
I just wanted you
because I never believed
I'd have you,
maybe I should have thought twice
& realized even Magic has its limits,
maybe I should have listened to the Moonlight
& gone dancing, amorous with another
summer smiling maiden, maybe I should have
done a thousand things & chased something
sensible for a change, but that's not who I am & who
I'll always be, I'm no Hero but I have a pilgrim's soul,
I know I'm on a journey & come danger, disaster or high water
in the end it's only the adventure that truly matters,
it's only those lost & desolate nights out in the desert
when the constellations flame across the Earth & phantoms & angels
own your heartbeat, I could have loved you & ended
a simple heartbroken fool but that's not the fate a poet's always granted,
we live & we live & we live again, I saw the galaxies
in your eyes & I felt the electricity of your bones, I knew the Goddess
was complex & cunning & exquisite to contemplate,
I knew you were unknowable, a child, a woman, a fleeting hint
of Mystery that would finally unravel my world, I knew your green eyes
were an ocean the Light would always break across, radiant with rainbows,
whispering, whispering, whispering of sensual fingertips
& butterfly wings upon our skin, I just undressed you & marvelled
at what I found, I was a fool but I'll never regret it, even out here
where the sunlight shimmers with easy Lovers, you were worth everything,
every wound, every scar, every pain,
every Ecstasy...

136

IN THE FIELDS OF MERCY

I was
just running, I guess,
I was just running
& the constellations found me,
I was just lost & bewildered,
almost to the point of madness, in the hopeless
ecstasy of all wild & wandering pilgrims,
you just lay me down, here in the last of the summer meadows,
here in the fields of Mercy, you just lay me down
& embraced me, even against my better judgment, you made me
the Hero I always thought I'd be, we slept as if we were
the last & most exquisite dream of the Cosmos,
dawn loved us but I think sensual Midnight loved us more,
you just kept asking me as if I knew the secret & I did somehow,
but only in your arms, I had a thousand words & they had wild wings,
I had a thousand words but they were never as profound
as the simplest of your whispers, you were always enough for me,
you were always exquisite enough to spark the galaxies within my atoms,
I knew no Magic except the sweet simple miracle of the blossoms
& the delicious slow dancing of the seasons, maybe I took you too fast
to those vast silences between our heartbeats where any miracle can happen,
you were always the Beauty who haunted me, yesterday, today & tomorrow,
maybe memories still have meaning but the river always flows,
what can I say, how many tears will fill this ocean, just remember me,
wherever you are, whether out amid the nebulae or so close
you could tap me on the shoulder, you were the quiet Lover who
somehow knew all the answers, you could look at me & break me,
you could touch me & I suddenly knew what Life was,

& what it meant to be human & naked
& beautiful beneath
the Stars...

A BEAUTIFUL MADNESS

Maybe
I'll meet you,
today, yesterday, or tomorrow,
maybe I'll meet you
& the moment won't elude us,
maybe the galaxies will shift & the Stars
will finally align, maybe I'll meet you,
out in that first & final field of rainbows,
maybe I'll dare to die & be reborn, at last in your arms,
maybe it'll almost be enough & the Cosmos
will loosen our strings, a least a little, maybe puppets
will gradually have their day & all pilgrims & long lost lovers
will slowly surrender, maybe one day a kiss will truly
be forever & the journeys of our flesh, fantasies & atoms
will finally be fulfilled, I keep thinking I see you, moment after moment
& eon after eon, I keep thinking that I see you & at last
we'll embrace longer than a heartbeat, deeper than the surface ecstasies
that seem so profound & yet so fleeting, we have to believe this
or all else is disaster, we have to believe this or Love is nothing
but a beautiful madness, a flicker of the fading Midnight wind
& a constant yearning of the morning, keep me where you least expect
to find me & perhaps that will finally set us free, we drift in this river
toward the sea of all possible Raptures, we drift & it's almost enough,
it's almost like Bliss will finally set us free, the current enfolds the nebulae
& the dance is always forever, it's only that here we are again,
human & childish in our innocence, it's only that
we somehow always know everything already,
but just keep smiling
& forgetting it...

A SMILE STILL LASTS FOREVER

I'll
still meet you,
if there's time & the Cosmos
wills it, if there's time I'll still
come to you, bold, bright, & Beautiful,
just as you imagined me, a thousand years ago,
if there's time I'll still tell you
one last story, one last legend of our Heartbeats,
I'll still come to you & I'll remember everything,
every kiss, every caress, every promise
we wrapped in imagined rainbows, if there's time
I'll still come riding across that skyline, I'll still reach you,
in that golden grove, in those sunlit grasses down by the river,
I'll still be young, at least in Spirit & my Heart
will at last be open, I'll come amid the blossoms in this last
& greatest springtime of our lives, I'll always be here for you,
I'll always just love you, love you, love you, deeper & more profoundly,
I'll just be the Lover you always dreamed I'd be,
my Life is a disaster & also my greatest triumph, I never know
how to judge it except by the shining in your eyes,
I was mortal, Magic, & the Midnight always led me onward,
I was everything I never thought I'd be & now I know what golden dust
truly tastes like, just forgive me & lead me homeward,
just believe in me one last time, as if I was still that young & beautiful
Hero you always dreamed I'd be, I'll just be here now if you'll still have me,
if I'm still strong enough to hold you, if I'm still fleet enough to free you
from this great coming of the Midnight & imminent dissolution
of the worlds, just believe me, just listen for me because

I've almost reached you, Summer lingers yet a moment longer,
& winter has promised to love us, at least
for a moment that smiles
& lasts forever...

BLUE EYES DANCING

Perhaps
there's still time,
perhaps tomorrow is never forever,
perhaps from amorous acorns
great oak trees still rise & gather long lost
constellations, perhaps these rusty keys still unlock
the rainbows, perhaps truth still shimmers,
somehow in the telling of these stories,
somehow in the endless lighting of these lonely campfires,
perhaps each whisper still holds the Magic,
the strange & subtle invitation to come out naked amid
the great rapture of the most exquisite of the Stars,
I just wander these endless highways once etched upon this desert
by seekers more miraculous & determined than I,
I just smile & watch you dancing, in a moment so unexpected
it was almost like the sunlight breaking at last across these endless
& unruly oceans, where you come from I know not & where you're going
I can only guess, to be honest I couldn't even see you coming,
Autumn is often a cool season of contemplation but a hint of subtle lightning
has been added now, I don't know what the Cosmos has in store for us
except this one simple & perfect moment, perhaps it's beautiful,
perhaps it's profound, but I'm ancient & I'm always wary,
Midnight is always dangerous, either in the here & now or sometime later,
when you least expect it, I just know I can't comprehend you,
you're almost giddy in your rhythms & yet you're always watching,
as if the river flows faster here & safety is an illusion,
it's as if the rapids are here now & pilgrims
must sink or swim...

A LOST GODDESS

Maybe
you gave me
something, maybe you
did & I never quite knew
what it was, maybe you gave me
something & I just lost it
when the west wind blew, so cool
& mysterious in across those wild waves
I'd always wondered about, maybe
you gave me something & perhaps it was
even Magic, maybe it was marvellous & maybe
I should have felt a little deeper, kissed a little longer
& looked a little closer, maybe I should have
seen beyond the obvious & understood you a little better,
perhaps I should have loved you just a little bit longer,
maybe I should have just let the Stars smile
& shatter all around us, maybe I should have been
content to just be your poet, your joker, your fool, maybe
I should have just realized that you were just wounded
& I was the amorous hunter who shot that cunning & irresistible arrow,
maybe I should have listened to your mysteries but never
to your whispers, maybe I should have just quietly come closer
instead of riding in so boldly, maybe I should have waited a little longer
before I gave you the most dangerous of my constellations,
maybe I should have just embraced the exquisite miracle of your skin
& just let your Spirit wander as the galaxies willed,
perhaps I never knew you, perhaps I always did, the Cosmos
smiled & brought you but it was Moonlight on the water that lured you
to the river, today still seems like yesterday back here where

we're both still waiting, even though we won't admit it
& keep our eyes so firmly fixed
on the horizon...

A WAKING MIRACLE

This dream
was holy, infinite,
this dream was the dream
we all secretly long for,
the blossom within each of our Hearts,
always aching to bloom & transform
this Earth in each waking miracle of our lives,
this dream was holy in that the Cosmos willed it,
as if the galaxies gathered & trembled
within me, as if the oceans were my bloodstream,
as if the winds were wild & no different from my breath,
I had that dream, that moment, that Magic,
shining within me & I knew it had always been there
& Light would still somehow always break across the meadows
& each shimmering of the dewdrops, I saw the nebulae
nestled within the exquisite eternity of my fingers, I heard
the rustle of the branches urging each bright leaf into the cleansing
arms of autumn, I heard it all, I saw it all, I felt the ecstasy
of each bright Beauty bequeathed me, I felt the flicker of each
fleeting kiss upon my lips, I danced, danced, danced
& each atom danced as if my heartbeat, this dream was holy,
as if the Universe smiled & saw itself revealed in each stone,
each raindrop, each wild wing across the sunrise, I saw you everywhere
& not just cradled in my arms so lightly as dawn still lingered in your hair,
I saw you everywhere & I knew that we lay here in the centre
of the world, as innocent as Lovers always are,
when Life is still so simple
& so profound…

MY MISSING PIECES

You were
always dangerous,
divine, holy, you were
always dangerous, & joyous
& profound, you were always graceful,
gliding through the meadows,
you were always trembling, as if in subtle
anticipation, as if the shimmering of a dewdrop
sublime in her ecstasy, you were always my guide,
my Lover, my saviour through each lost & lonely nightfall,
where phantoms danced you always found me
& Spirited me away, I was never so damaged you could not heal me,
I was never so broken you could not find my missing pieces,
I always returned to you, no matter how wildly I wandered,
no matter how unruly the waters I sailed upon nor how strange
the kingdoms I found myself living in, I always had the Stars
& the miracle of your kiss, & I never knew which blessing was the greater,
I always had the electricity of your fingertips like the tingle
of erotic butterflies amid my atoms, you always knew me,
you always saw right through me, in you I saw the Light, the holy halo
of each heartbeat granted, in you I saw the journey & the Hero's final return,
to where each of us began, here in the smile of the Cosmos
& the sudden strange hush of the nebulae, you were everything to me
& I was hardly worthy, just forgive this child, this joker, this fool,
I brought a thousand gifts for you but they were never what you wanted,
I was born to Love you & this is the purest treasure I hope to give you,
I was a simple man but I let the glitter & bright ghosts fool me,
I could have been better but at least I was no worse, just accept me

& forgive me, I've dreamed of you forever, just redeem me,
just forgive me, just believe me
now at last...

ONLY POETS KNOW

I guess
I sought you,
in all those unknown
& miraculous places that only
poets know, I guess I sought you in those
subtle storms of the Spirit
that dance so intimately with Midnight,
I guess I sought you in those sensuous groves
out in the wild wood where satyrs
& nymphs still kiss in erotic sunbeams,
I guess I sought you in the innocence that seems
to still sustain me, in each beating of my Heart,
whether the Stars were smiling or just quietly laughing I guess
I'll never know, I believed in you & I believed in the journey,
I bore each ecstasy, each hardship, each Loving wound
as if it was sacred & some sort of secret miracle,
I guess the dawn believed in me because it always rose
& revealed the Earth & all its ancient wonders,
each morning I was born again & somewhere in each coming
of the twilight the phantoms embraced me once again,
a thousand times I thought I'd found you, each kiss completed me
& calmed the trembling of my bloodstream, each embrace
caressed me with the electric spark of newborn galaxies,
I always sought you, as if you guided me, as if you sought me
with the erotic fervour of the nebulae, I never forgot that I was dust
& Light & bone, I never forgot that the abyss & I are one, & that my destiny
begins & ends at last with the atoms, just lie with me a moment, Love,
before the next storm rises & sweeps away our world,

perhaps I'm a Hero, perhaps I'm a madman, but in the end I think
I'm just a human, one of us & all of us,
just like we all are…

IN THE CRADLE OF THIS MORNING

Here
in the cradle
of this Morning,
in the shimmering of this
early Light, all things begin again,
yesterday's dreams were yesterday's dreams
& owe nothing to tomorrow,
here in the cradle of this morning
Beauty lies yet a moment longer before rising
to embrace the full coming of this day,
the little things matter now, the softness of your breathing,
the exquisite tendrils of your hair drifting
so lightly across my chest, here in the cradle of this morning
the Cosmos is subtle & sweet & shimmers within us,
the seas lie quiet & all storms are forgotten until they gather,
I could lie like this forever & still it would never be
long enough, whatever truth I need I always find it here,
whatever Love, whatever gentle reminder to enjoy the journey
in the ecstasy of its moments, here in the cradle of this morning
my Spirit rests unshaken & Rapture finally seems
gently within my fingertips, perhaps we're born to struggle,
to rise & fall & rise again, to journey always toward the horizon,
perhaps that's who we are but I never quite believe it,
I never quite believe that's what the rainbows truly whisper,
if Joy is a mystic thing then I willingly embrace its Mystery in each
eternity when I kiss you, if the true oceans are between our bloodstreams
then I willing sail them just to glimpse you, immaculate
in your inner constellations, all is holy here, sacred in the fragrance

of the blossoms drifting in through our open window,
the world is here, & all the treasures
of this Earth...

Made in the USA
Columbia, SC
25 August 2018